Praying with the Saints by Season: Winter

PRAYING WITH THE SAINTS BY SEASON

WINTER

FR. PATRICK TROADEC, SSPX

Translated by Michael J. Miller
and Susan Treacy

PO Box 217 | Saint Marys, KS 66536

Original edition, *Prier un hiver avec les saints au jour le jour* (Versailles: Via Romana, 2017)

Translated from the French by Michael J. Miller and Susan Treacy.

Cover: *Winter in Switzerland*, 1850, Francis Jasper Cropsey (1823-1900)

Library of Congress Control Number: 2022946450

© 2023 Angelus Press
All rights reserved.

ANGELUS PRESS
PO Box 217
Saint Marys, Kansas 66536
Phone (816) 753-3150
Fax (816) 753-3557
Order Line (800) 966-7337
www.angeluspress.org

ISBN: 978-1-68529-026-9
FIRST PRINTING—September 2023

Printed in the United States of America

Table of Contents

Note to the Reader _____ 1
The Saints Selected _____ 2

St. Thomas (Dec. 21) _____ 4
St. Frances Xavier Cabrini (Dec. 22) _____ 6
St. Ivo of Chartres (Dec. 23) _____ 8
Blessed Jacopone (Dec. 24) _____ 11
Christmas (Dec. 25) _____ 13
St. Stephen (Dec. 26) _____ 15
St. John the Evangelist (Dec. 27) _____ 17
Holy Innocents (Dec. 28) _____ 19
St. Thomas Becket (Dec. 29) _____ 21
Blessed Alain de Solminihac (Dec. 30) _____ 24
St. Sylvester (Dec. 31) _____ 27
Holy Resolutions (Jan. 1) _____ 29
The Holy Name of Jesus (Jan. 2) _____ 31
St. Genevieve (Jan. 3) _____ 34
St. Angela of Foligno (Jan. 4) _____ 36
St. Simeon Stylites (Jan. 5) _____ 38
Epiphany – The Three Kings (Jan. 6) _____ 40
The Holy Family (The Sunday after Jan. 6) _____ 43
Jesus, Model of Poverty (Jan. 8) _____ 45
Jesus, Model of Charity (Jan. 9) _____ 48
Jesus, Model of Purity (Jan. 10) _____ 51
Jesus, Model of Obedience (Jan. 11) _____ 53
Jesus, Source of Joy (Jan. 12) _____ 55
The Baptism of Jesus (Jan. 13) _____ 57
St. Hilary (Jan. 14) _____ 59
St. Paul, The First Hermit (Jan. 15) _____ 61
St. Marcellus (Jan. 16) _____ 64

Praying with the Saints: Winter

St. Anthony, Abbot (Jan. 17)	66
St. Margaret of Hungary (Jan. 18)	68
Our Lady of Pontmain (Jan. 19)	70
St. Sebastian (Jan. 20)	72
St. Agnes (Jan. 21)	74
St. Vincent (Jan. 22)	76
St. Raymond of Peñafort (Jan. 23)	79
St. Timothy (Jan. 24)	82
The Conversion of St. Paul (Jan. 25)	85
St. Polycarp (Jan. 26)	88
St. John Chrysostom (Jan. 27)	90
St. Peter Nolasco (Jan. 28)	92
St. Francis de Sales (Jan. 29)	94
St. Martina (Jan. 30)	96
St. John Bosco (Jan. 31)	98
St. Ignatius of Antioch (Feb. 1)	100
The Presentation of Jesus at the Temple (Feb. 2)	103
St. Blaise (Feb. 3)	106
St. Joan of France (Feb. 4)	108
St. Agatha (Feb. 5)	110
St. Dorothy (Feb. 6)	112
St. Romuald (Feb. 7)	114
St. John of Matha (Feb. 8)	116
St. Cyril of Alexandria (Feb. 9)	118
St. Scholastica (Feb. 10)	120
Our Lady of Lourdes (Feb. 11)	122
The Seven Founders of the Servites (Feb. 12)	124
St. Catherine de Ricci (Feb. 13)	126
St. Valentine (Feb. 14)	128
Saints Faustinus and Jovita (Feb. 15)	130
St. Juliana of Nicomedia (Feb. 16)	132
Blessed Henry Suso (Feb. 17)	134
St. Bernadette (Feb. 18)	136

Table of Contents

St. Margaret of Cortona (Feb. 19)	138
Jacinta of Fatima (Feb. 20)	140
Blessed Noël Pinot (Feb. 21)	142
The Chair of St. Peter (Feb. 22)	145
St. Peter Damian (Feb. 23)	147
St. Matthias (Feb. 24)	149
Blessed Sebastian of Aparicio (Feb. 25)	151
St. Porphyry of Gaza (Feb. 26)	154
St. Gabriel of the Sorrowful Mother (Feb. 27)	156
Blessed Antonia (Feb. 28)	159
St. Albinus (Alvin) (Mar. 1)	161
St. Paphnutius (Mar. 2)	163
St. Winwaloe (Guénolé) (Mar. 3)	165
St. Casimir (Mar. 4)	167
St. John Joseph of the Cross (Mar. 5)	169
Saints Perpetua and Felicity (Mar. 6)	171
St. Thomas Aquinas (Mar. 7)	173
St. John of God (Mar. 8)	176
St. Frances of Rome (Mar. 9)	178
The Forty Martyrs of Sebaste (Mar. 10)	180
St. Pol of Léon (Mar. 11)	182
St. Gregory the Great (Mar. 12)	184
St. Euphrasia (Mar. 13)	186
St. Matilda (Mar. 14)	188
St. Louise de Marillac (Mar. 15)	190
The Holy Canadian Martyrs (Mar. 16)	193
St. Patrick (Mar. 17)	196
St. Cyril of Jerusalem (Mar. 18)	199
St. Joseph (1) (Mar. 19)	201
St. Joseph (2) (Mar. 20)	203

Prayers

Spiritual Communion	206
The Mysteries of the Rosary	207
The Apostles' Creed	208
An Act of Faith	209
An Act of Hope	209
An Act of Charity	209
An Act of Contrition	209
The Memorare of St. Bernard	210
Litany of Humility	210
Litany of the Precious Blood	211
Litany of the Sacred Heart	213
Latin Prayers	215

Bibliography _____ 219

Note to the Reader

Dear Reader,

A series of little meditation books corresponding to the different seasons of the liturgical year was published in French by Via Romana. We continue the series now with booklets that present the lives of the saints who are celebrated by the Church—here, the ones celebrated in winter. The presentation is identical to the one in the preceding volumes. For each day a citation from Sacred Scripture is provided, followed by a summary of the life or the praises of the saint of the day.

Two thoughts, expressed by the saint himself or related to his life, help to foster meditation. In order for it to produce abundant, concrete, and lasting fruits, one or two prayers and three resolutions are also offered for each day; the whole presentation takes less than two pages.

So that the reader can recognize the saints when they visit churches or museums, the booklet often notes their attributes and emblems. It also describes their patronage and the circumstances in which they are customarily invoked.

Finally, in order to foster piety, while remaining in the spirit of the meditation, several prayers and canticles are added as an appendix to the volume.

"Anyone who wishes to become perfect in the practice of the virtues must study the lives of the saints, as so many living, practical models, and then, by diligent imitation, take possession of the good that is found in them."[1] And St. Francis de Sales explained: "What are the lives of the saints if not the Gospel put into action? There is no more difference between the written Gospel and the lives of the saints than between a piece of music that is *noted* and one that is *sung*."[2] The saints are true artists, who interpret very accu-

---

[1] St. Basile, *Sermon I sur la vertu et le vice*, in: *Oeuvres complètes*, III/2, chap. 5 (Paris: Gaume, 1839), 691.

[2] Letter dated October 5, 1604, to Monseigneur André Frémyot, Archbishop of Bourges, *Oeuvres complètes*, Éditions d'Annecy, 306.

rately the inspired melodies that are *noted* in Sacred Scripture. Thus their lives appear like a prelude to the sounds of the eternal hymns sung in unison by the choirs of angels and of the elect.

The saints lived in various eras, in very different situations, but they are close to us because of their attractiveness and are just waiting for our prayers in order to help us. Besides the better known saints, this booklet introduces many others who also deserve our admiration, veneration, and to a certain extent imitation.

While meditating on their lives attentively and with devotion, you will feel very small in comparison to them, but at the same time you will feel encouraged to become better, especially if you follow this valuable advice given by Monsignor Ghika: "The best way to celebrate the saints is to resemble them. Why not try to live as they did, if only for one day, *their* day, the day consecrated and blessed by the Church, when they are 'on duty' to help us?"[3]

Assuring you of my priestly prayers, especially during the celebration of the Holy Sacrifice of the Mass, I commend myself to yours and thank you very much in advance.

Father Patrick Troadec

The Saints Selected

Every day the Church commemorates a large number of saints listed in the Roman Martyrology. In more than six out of ten cases, the one celebrated by the Universal Church (1962 Missal) was chosen. The other saints were selected from among the commemorations proper to certain localities or religious communities. When two important saints are celebrated on the same day, the life of the second one has been shifted to a feria close to the feast.

---

[3] Prince Vladimir Ghika, *Pensées pour la suite des jours* (Paris: Beauchesne, 1962), 172.

Note to the Reader

Most of them lived in the early Christian centuries, but all the periods of Church history are represented. Among the saints from the Renaissance to the contemporary period, some are well known, such as Francis de Sales, John Bosco, Bernadette Soubirous, and Jacinta of Fatima, while others deserve to be, such as Blesseds Sebastian of Aparicio (O.F.M.) and Alain de Solminihac, or Saints John of God, John-Joseph of the Cross (O.F.M.), Catherine de Ricci (O.P.), and Frances-Xavier Cabrini.

Every day the Church commemorates the martyrs in her liturgy to encourage the faithful to carry their cross and follow the Divine Master. The French martyrs who died in Canada in the 17th century and Blessed Noël Pinot, who died during the French Revolution, are honored in this volume to recall that every era has its martyrs.

To the saints who died *in odio fidei* [victims of hatred for the Faith], the Church joins an impressive array of virgins, confessors, and doctors. Some died in the flower of their youth (Jacinta, Agnes, Gabriel of the Sorrowful Mother, Vincent), others after a long life (Anthony the Hermit, Raymond of Peñafort, Romuald). They came from all social circles and from widely different nationalities. Many come from Italy (24 saints), France (14), Asia Minor (present-day Turkey) (10), and Palestine (9). The others are of Sicilian, Greek, Spanish, Portuguese, British, German, Hungarian, Polish, Egyptian, Tunisian, and Canadian origin.

Although many of the blessed showed signs of sanctity at a very early age (Bernadette, Euphrasia), others went through a period of lukewarmness (Angela of Foligno, Romuald), or of sin (Margaret of Cortona). Thus, in the course of reading these pages, everyone will be able to discover a saint within reach.

In order to stay in the liturgical spirit appropriate for the Christmas season, from January 8 to 12 the meditations concern several virtues of Jesus that the saints admired and reproduced in their lives.

St. Thomas

December 21

GOD SPEAKS TO US

"Because thou hast seen Me, Thomas, thou hast believed: blessed are they that have not seen and have believed."

—John 20:29

MEDITATION

A fisherman from Galilee, Thomas had the honor of hearing Jesus invite him to join the 12 Apostles. His name in Hebrew means "twin"; the Greek word for it is Didymus. St. John mentions three times when he intervened: when Our Lord decided to return to Judea to visit Lazarus, he said he was ready to die with Him, thus revealing his great courage and his devotion. During the discourse after the Last Supper, he asked Jesus the way so as to follow Him (Jn. 14:5). After the resurrection of Jesus, when the other Apostles report to him that they had been blessed by an apparition of Jesus, he exclaimed, "Except I shall see in His hands the print of the nails and put my finger into the place of the nails and put my hand into His side, I will not believe" (Jn. 20:25). But then, one week later, Jesus reappeared to His Apostles, and walking straight to Thomas, He said to him: "Put in thy finger hither and see My hands. And bring hither thy hand and put it into My side. And be not faithless, but believing" (Jn. 20:27). What a humiliation for Thomas to receive this apparition in the presence of the other Apostles! But at the same time, what a joy! These two feelings of extreme embarrassment and immense joy are present in him. Confronted with the evidence and at the same time facing such a mark of condescension and love on the part of Our Lord, he could only exclaim: "My Lord and my God" (Jn. 20:28). After Pentecost, when the Apostles divided up the world, the countries of the Parthians, Medes, and Persians fell to his lot. He even went as far as India and was martyred in Mylapore, near Madras.

St. Thomas

"O St. Thomas, we do not ask to see clearly, but for simple, docile faith; for He Who comes for us, too, told you when He showed Himself to you: 'Blessed are they that have not seen and have believed!' We want to be in their number."[4] "Obtain for us a share in your faith so that we might exclaim before the manger: 'My Lord and my God.'"

Attributes and patronage

St. Thomas is depicted with a lance because of his martyrdom, or with a carpenter's square, or else receiving the belt of Our Lady as she went up to heaven. He is the patron saint of India.

Prayer

Grant us, we beseech Thee, O Lord, to glory in the solemn feast of Thy Blessed Apostle Thomas, that we may ever be helped by his patronage and follow his faith with suitable devotion. (Collect)

Thoughts

- "My God, how blind man is, unless he opens his heart to the light of faith!"

  —St. Bernadette, L, 1875.

- "God will not permit anyone to lose the Faith while working to bring it to others."

  —Curé of Ars, PPJ1, December 22

Resolutions

1 Recite an act of faith. (See appendix.)

2 Make reparation by fidelity to your duty for blasphemies and indifference toward God by starting with what costs you the most.

3 Work for the religious revival of your country by showing that you are proud to be a Catholic and by leading a life that is in keeping with the Faith.

---

[4] Dom Guéranger, *AL, TA* p. 543.

St. Frances Xavier Cabrini

December 22

GOD SPEAKS TO US

Thou hast held me by my right hand; and by Thy will Thou hast conducted me: and with Thy glory Thou hast received me.
—Introit: Psalm 72:24

MEDITATION

The 19th century witnessed a wealth of new religious congregations. Among the foundresses, one Italian woman stands out: Frances Xavier Cabrini (1850-1917).

The 13th child of a farming family, she was born in Lombardy (Italy). At the age of 13 she made a vow of virginity. A schoolteacher at the age of 22, she dreamed of going off to the missions in China. However, no congregation would accept her because of her frail health. In 1874, the parish priest in Codogno entrusted to her an orphanage that had been mismanaged. Three years later, the bishop closed it, allowed her to pursue her interest in the missions, and invited her to start an Institute in keeping with her desires.

So it was in 1880 she founded together with six friends the Congregation of the Missionary Sisters of the Sacred Heart. However, Pope Leo XIII did not permit her to travel to China, but rather to the United States to help the Italian immigrants who had recently settled there. The community was designed to provide for the education of girls in Catholic, Protestant, or pagan countries. Whereas the Rule prescribed four hours of prayer per day, she would get up an hour before the other sisters to pray more.

The Italian immigrants needed support. In the vicinity of New York City, for example, there were 50,000 of them. Many had fallen into poverty, material and moral. It was suggested that she open an orphanage and an elementary school, but the Archbishop of New York was opposed to the idea at first, to her great disappointment. She stood firm, and finally opened the orphanage. In 1892 a hospital was founded in the same city. Then the foundress extended her apostolate to South America. She opened a secondary school for girls in Buenos Aires (Argentina), then in 1914 created an orphanage in France, in Noisy-le-Grand, for the daughters of Italian immigrants.

In 1907, when the constitutions were approved, the congregation already had a thousand nuns.

She died in Chicago, ten years later, exhausted but happy to have performed her duty to the end, leaving 30 religious houses in eight countries. Pope Pius XII canonized her in 1946.

Prayer

O Lord Jesus Christ, Thou didst inflame with the fire of Thy most Sacred Heart the holy Virgin Frances Xavier, and didst lead her through the widest regions of the world to win souls for Thee, and by means of her raised up a new family in Thy Church; grant, we beseech Thee, that through her intercession we may be imbued with the virtues of Thy Sacred Heart and be worthy to reach the haven of eternal happiness. (Collect)

Thoughts

- "The humblest soul is the one most loved by the Heart of Jesus."

  —St. Frances Xavier Cabrini, SMP, p. 16

- "May your face always be serene, joyful, so that it inspires peace in everyone you meet."

  —St. Frances Xavier Cabrini, SMP, p. 62

Resolutions

1. Recite a decade of the Rosary so that children who are not practicing the Faith may celebrate a truly Christian Christmas.

2. Recite several times a day the invocation, "Jesus, meek and humble of heart, make my heart like Thine."

3. Render service spontaneously for the love of God.

St. Ivo of Chartres

December 23

GOD SPEAKS TO US

And now, ye kings, understand: receive instruction, you that judge the earth.... Embrace discipline: lest at any time the Lord be angry, and you perish from the just way.

—Psalm 2:10, 12

MEDITATION

Born in Auteuil, in the region of Beauvais, Ivo or "Yves" (1040-1116) was blessed to have good parents who raised him to be straightforward and pious. They sent him to be educated at the Benedictine abbey in Bec (Normandy). Ivo decided to dedicate himself to God and became a priest, then a Master in canon law. Both an instructor and a writer, he composed two works in which he supported the doctrinal infallibility of the Pope, and affirmed and substantiated his rights against the abusive interference of the kings. Ivo succeeded Geoffroy, a simoniac bishop (who had acquired his office for a sum of money). He was consecrated by Pope Urban II, who encouraged him by telling him: "Keep the faith of Christ pure and spotless. Never let yourself be driven by the winds of prosperity, not downcast by setbacks, and set your heart on higher things than human events."

No sooner was he ordained than he had to confront a storm stirred up by the King of France, Philip I. The latter had been married for 22 years to Bertha of Holland, by whom he had had two children; he banished the Queen to a convent and abducted the young Bertrade de Montfort, the legitimate wife of the Count of Anjou. When he was invited to the sacrilegious ceremony of their marriage, Ivo replied to the king: "In no way can I give such scandal to the Christian people. Remember the example of Solomon. Beware of falling with him and losing your earthly kingdom and the eternal kingdom as well." Furious, the king ordered that Ivo be thrown into prison; two years later he finally released Ivo, yet without separating from Bertrade, with whom he later had two sons. When Hugh of Lyons, the Apostolic Legate supported by Ivo, was about to excommunicate the King and his concubine, Queen Bertha died of grief. The Archbishops of Rheims, Sens, and Tours then met in a council in Rheims where they accused Ivo of the felony crime of treason against the king.

Nevertheless, with the passage of time, the king at last decided to be reconciled with the Church. Bertrade left the court, and Philip asked Ivo to inform Urban II of this fact and to initiate proceedings for the purpose of a reconciliation. At the Council of Beaugency, Philip and Bertrade promised on the book of the Holy Gospels to renounce their guilty liaison. Bertrade, soon moved by the words of a holy monk, repented and left the court forever. The king and Bertrade were absolved in 1104, and Ivo then continued his work as a valiant, faithful, and prudent pastor until his death.

Prayer

Be with us, Lord, and free us, appeased by the intercession of Thy blessed Bishop Ivo, whom Thou didst set up in Thy house as a burning, shining lamp. (Collect)

Thoughts

- "For God hath not given us the spirit of fear: but of power and of love and of sobriety."

    —II Timothy 1:7

- "Be not deceived: God is not mocked. For what things a man shall sow, those also shall he reap. For he that soweth in his flesh, of the flesh also shall reap corruption. But he that soweth in the spirit, of the spirit shall reap life everlasting.

    —Galatians 6:7-8

Resolutions

1. Pray to God to raise up holy bishops in your country.
2. Defend Christian marriage and its indissolubility against the permissive morality currently in vogue.
3. In order to become stronger in the virtue of fortitude, resolve to be faithful to the duties of your state in life until the end.

Blessed Jacopone

December 24

GOD SPEAKS TO US

Now there stood by the cross of Jesus, his mother and his mother's sister, Mary of Cleophas, and Mary Magdalen.
—John 19:25

MEDITATION

Jacopone (Jacob, James) de Benedetti (*ca.* 1230-1306) was born in Todi, in Umbria (Italy). He studied grammar, rhetoric, and jurisprudence at the University of Bologna and earned a doctorate in civil law. He loved entertainment and led a superficial life. He married Vanna Donna, a rich and virtuous young woman. During one festival, Vanna fell to the ground, dead, and Jacob then discovered a coarse hair shirt beneath her rich garments. This incident was for him a genuine revelation. In a split second he realized the vanity of earthly things and firmly resolved to abandon frivolous pleasures. After distributing his property to the poor, he entered the Secular Franciscan Order, and as a result children called him "Jacopone," "crazy Jake." In search of a more austere life, he knocked at the door of the Friars Minor in his native town. They took him in with some reservations, but soon were favorably impressed by his comportment.

Jacopone was truly filled with love for God, which led him to sing His praises during his nature walks or else to compose poetry. He was so detached that he said that when God did not grant what he asked for in prayer, he was twice as glad.

He drew his love of God from his deep humility. And so he considered himself unworthy of the priesthood. Once he became a religious, he kept the nickname Jacopone, which had at first been given to ridicule him.

Despite his mortification, it sometimes happened that he remembered his past and felt nostalgic about it. And so, in order to overcome that temptation, he took a piece of meat to his cell and let it spoil there, saying to himself: "This is what you dared to take as your ideal!"

At that time, Pope St. Peter Celestine resigned from the papacy, and Boniface VIII replaced him. Misinformed, Blessed Jacopone sided with the enemies of the Pope, which earned him excommunication and even imprisonment. Under the next successor, Benedict XI, he was set free.

Over the course of the year 1306 he fell seriously ill and was warned of his impending death. Then he summoned his close friend John of La Verna, who remained at his bedside until his soul had flown to heaven.

The Blessed Franciscan left to us, among other poems, the beautiful Sequence *Stabat Mater*. From time immemorial the Church has venerated him.

Prayer

Holy Mother, pierce me through, in my heart each wound renew of my Savior Crucified.... Be to me, O Virgin, nigh, lest in flames I burn and die, in His awful judgment day. Christ, when Thou shalt call me hence, be Thy Mother my defense; be Thy cross my victory.

—*Stabat Mater*

Thoughts

- "Is there one who would not weep, 'whelmed in miseries so deep, Christ's dear Mother to behold?"

  —*Stabat Mater*

- "For the sins of His own nation, [she] saw Him hang in desolation."

  —*Stabat Mater*

Resolutions

1 Recite or sing the *Stabat Mater*. (See appendix.)

2 Stay recollected as much as possible during the day, and don't get anxious about Christmas preparations.

3 During the day, read the Gospel for Midnight Mass.

Christmas

December 25

GOD SPEAKS TO US

The shepherds said one to another: Let us go over to Bethlehem and let us see this word that is come to pass which the Lord hath shewed to us.

—Mass at Dawn: Luke 2:15

MEDITATION

What a marvelous night was that night in Bethlehem! A night that is dark only for those who are asleep! An obscure night for the rationalistic mind that wants to understand everything! A gloomy night for those who are bogged down in the pleasures of life!

A luminous night, on the other hand, for those who have a sense of mystery! A radiant night for those who are nostalgic for a kind of greatness that is beyond them and that God alone can offer them! A dazzling night for those whose hearts are filled with hope and know that they are loved by God, infinitely loved! O sweet night! O holy night!

The shepherds, not knowing what name to give to the news that they had just learned through the intervention of the angels, speak about "the word that is come to pass." This is indeed the language of simple folk, of modest, uneducated people—the language of shepherds. By itself, the very natural simplicity of the account would testify to the fidelity of the gospel narrator in whom the Blessed Virgin Mary confided.

St. Luke did not have to prove that God exists; that was a truth that everyone admitted. However, he had to prove to us that God loves us, that we no longer have to seek Him because He came to us: He descended from heaven.

The shepherds who came that night to pay Him homage would perhaps never know that the Child of Bethlehem would proudly say one day: "I am the good shepherd" (Jn. 10:11).[5]

O Jesus, You were born in Bethlehem, a name that means "House of Bread." You are the living bread that came down from heaven. I want to be united to You by receiving You fervently in Holy Communion.

Prayer

Grant, we beseech Thee, O Lord our God, that we, who rejoice in celebrating these mysteries of the Nativity of our Lord Jesus Christ, may by a holy life become worthy someday to share the glory of heaven with Him. (Postcommunion of Midnight Mass)
Or
Grant, we beseech Thee, almighty God, that the new birth of Thine Only-begotten Son as man may set us free, who are held by the old bondage under the yoke of sin. (Collect of the Mass during the Day)

Thoughts

- "The Lamb gives Himself to the shepherds. Mary presents Him to them. How they hug Him in their arms, on their heart! O Mary, keep Jesus in my heart."
  —St. Bernadette, *CNI*, p. 368.

- "This feast of Christmas speaks so much to the soul: it seems that Jesus is inviting me to a new life, a life of love. Oh! If only I could be as little as He and then grow up at His side, setting my feet in His divine footsteps!"
  —Elizabeth of the Trinity, *PPJ*, December 25

Resolutions

1 Pray for a moment in front of the manger.
2 Offer your Holy Communion for the conversion of a sinner.
3 Recite the *Gloria in excelsis Deo*.

---

[5] Based on a homily by Msgr. Chevrot, À *l'écoute du Seigneur*, cassette n. 6 (Téqui).

St. Stephen

December 26

GOD SPEAKS TO US

Come, let us adore the newborn Christ, Who crowned St. Stephen this day.

—Matins: Invitatory Antiphon

MEDITATION

Why did the Church choose to honor this saint on this day? No doubt because of his eminent sanctity, but also because St. Stephen is the first martyr.

Indeed, the sign of the cross already appears on the day after Our Lord's birth to show that He came to earth as a propitiatory victim. From the moment of His incarnation, Jesus offers Himself to His Father as a victim to make reparation for our sins. We cannot separate Our Lord from His cross.

And the story of St. Stephen shows us that neither can we separate a Christian from the cross. St. Stephen demonstrated outstanding virtues during his life. He showed prudence in managing the property of the Church; he proved to have a fine spirit of detachment in his spiritual direction of widows; and above all he showed fortitude. This virtue appeared already during his preaching, which was so convincing for well-disposed souls that it aroused the hatred of his enemies. Indeed, exasperated by what they heard, the Jews, "crying out with a loud voice, stopped their ears and with one accord ran violently upon him." And finally, swept away by their rage, they seized him, "and casting him forth without the city, they stoned him" (Acts 7:58).

In these tragic circumstances, St. Stephen demonstrated his fortitude by patience, courageously accepting this hail of stones. He also showed his charity by forgiving his executioners and, even better, by praying for their conversion.

O St. Stephen, you went so far as to lay down your life for Our Lord; help me to witness in turn to the truths of the Faith without letting myself be intimidated by aggressive persons, and to forgive my neighbor so that someday I may share your happiness in heaven.

Attributes, Invocation, and Patronage

St. Stephen is depicted as a deacon carrying the rocks with which he was stoned. He is invoked for cases of headache. He is the patron saint of bricklayers and stonemasons.

Prayer

Grant us, we beseech Thee, O Lord, to imitate what we revere, that we may learn to love even our enemies, for we celebrate the heavenly birthday of him who knew how to pray for his very persecutors to Our Lord, Jesus Christ. (Collect)

Or

Great St. Stephen, obtain for me the grace to follow your example, by bearing patiently all the insults of my enemies, and to pray for them with a sincere heart, without desiring vengeance, so that on the day of my death, Jesus Christ, according to His promise, may pardon my sins.

—*Hours of Besançon*, printed by J. Lecoq, Troyes, 1546

Thoughts

- "Spiritual battles put us at the foot of the cross, and the cross puts us at the door of heaven."
 —The Curé of Ars, *PPJ2*, November 12

- "The Holy Ghost is a strong force.... He is the one who sustained the martyrs. Without the Holy Ghost, the martyrs would have fallen like leaves from the trees."
 —The Curé of Ars, *PPJ2*, October 26

Resolutions

1 Read the Epistle for the day.
2 Clearly state your identity as a Catholic when charity demands it.
3 Forgive from the bottom of your heart those who have done us wrong.

St. John the Evangelist

December 27

God speaks to us

Peter, turning about, saw that disciple whom Jesus loved following, who also leaned on His breast at supper.

—John 21:20

Meditation

St. John received three gifts from Jesus, three gifts that correspond to Our Lord's three states.

Our Lord indeed experienced three different states on this earth: life, death, and at the Last Supper an intermediate state, in which "He was a mixture of death and life, in which He was entirely both dead and alive; during the celebration of the Last Supper, when He ate with His disciples and showed them that He was alive; and when He wished to be eaten by His disciples, like an immolated sacrifice and seemed to them as though dead."[6]

During each of these states that Our Lord experienced, St. John received a corresponding gift. During Our Lord's life, St. John received from His Master the cross; at His death, he received from Him His Mother; and on Holy Thursday evening, at the Last Supper, St. John received the Heart of his Divine Master.

"You shall indeed drink of My chalice, and you will be baptized with My baptism" (*cf.* Mk. 10:39), Jesus said to His favorite disciple: that was the first present.

"Behold thy Mother" (Jn. 19:27), He declared to John from the cross: this is the second present.

And on Holy Thursday evening, He granted him the extraordinary privilege of resting his head on His chest so as to let John hear the beating of His heart, so as to make him experience the breadth of the divine love. This is the third present.

---

[6] Bossuet, "Panégyrique de saint Jean" (1658), *Oeuvres oratoires*, 2:527.

Lord Jesus, imitating St. John, I agree to carry my cross after You; I want to live as a child of Mary and to be a devotee of Your divine Heart. Every since my Baptism I have had access to Your Sacred Heart. On account of this, I promise to show my gratitude not only by my prayers, but also by my acts.

Attribute, invocation, and patronage

In iconography, St. John is depicted by an eagle. He is invoked against burns and poisoning and in order to preserve a good friendship. He is the patron saint of theologians and writers.

Prayer

Blessed disciple, Jesus loved you with a love that was well pleased. Tell him to love me at least with a love that is compassionate.
—Fr. Hyacinthe-Marie Cormier, *AS*, p. 367

Or

Lord, sweeten my heart with the sweetness of Yours!
—St. Francis de Sales, *PPJ*, December 13

Thoughts

- "What a truly happy disciple, to whom Jesus Christ gave His cross, so as to associate him to His suffering life; to whom Jesus Christ gave His Mother, so as to live eternally in his remembrance; to whom Jesus Christ gave His Heart, so that he might be one with Him forever after!"

  —Bossuet, *OEO*, 2:528-529

- "Jesus loved [St. John], because the special privilege of chastity had made him worthy of such a great love."
  —Matins: 2nd response of the 2nd nocturne

Resolutions

1 Offer one sacrifice a day to please Our Lord.

2 Pray your rosary with devotion.

3 Recite the litanies of the Sacred Heart. (See appendix.)

Holy Innocents

December 28

GOD SPEAKS TO US

Herod, perceiving that he was deluded by the wise men, was exceeding angry; and sending killed all the men children that were in Bethlehem and in all the borders thereof, from two years old and under, according to the time which he had diligently inquired of the wise men.

—Matthew 2:16

MEDITATION

Let us return to Bethlehem to venerate the Holy Innocents. Let us go to meet them so as to learn lessons from their unjust but glorious death. As St. Augustine says, "iniquity abounded against these blessed children, but even greater graces and heavenly blessings were poured out upon them... Those whom the impiousness of Herod snatched from the breast of their mothers who were still nursing them, are with good reason called the flowers of the martyrs: flowers that blossomed in the midst of the cold of disbelief."[7]

Fr. Emmanuel tells us:[8] "They are put to death for Jesus, and Jesus gives them eternal life. The Infant Jesus is glorified by the blood of these Holy Innocents, who have the honor of dying for Jesus: for Jesus Who would die for them and for us.

"If the angels of heaven could envy us something, it would be the ability to suffer for Jesus. For they cannot do this. They have the merit of innocence, of perfect purity: they do not have the merit of suffering.

"God revealed this to us sinners; and here are children who not only can suffer but, what is more, can die for the honor of God. Happy children, how beautiful is your lot! Pray to Jesus for us, and obtain for us the ability to suffer something for Him."

---

[7] Based on St. Augustine, *Sermon CCXX*, in *Oeuvres complètes*, vol. XX (Paris: Vivès, 1873), 379.

[8] Père Emmanuel, *Méditations* (Dismas, 1987), 30.

Patronage

The feast of the Holy Innocents is often the feast of novices so as to remind them that it is necessary to proclaim the glory of Christ, as these children did, not by words, but by their witness of death to the world and to the old man.

Prayer

Hail, O flowers of the martyrs, who, at the very threshold of life, were harvested by Christ's persecutor, as a whirlwind carries off rosebuds. You are the first victims of Christ, a tender flock of immolated children.

—Hymn at Lauds

Or

O flowers of the martyrs! Pray that we may have simplicity, a childlike heart, the naive confidence in God that does His will to the very end. Obtain for us the grace to carry our cross calmly when He sends it to us; that we may desire only His good pleasure.

—Dom Guéranger, *AL*, 2:415

Thoughts

- "The infinite merits of Our Lord Jesus Christ are more than sufficient to drown the crimes of the whole universe. Let us turn to Mary, who is the safe port of those who have made shipwreck, the hope of those who are hopeless."

    —Pauline Jaricot, *PPJ*, December 28

- "So many bitter trials, so many tokens of love."

    —Padre Pio, *FFN*, 16

Resolutions

1 Accept the day's contradictions in expiation for your sins.

2 Defend life from the moment of conception and denounce the crime of abortion.

3 Practice the virtue of purity vigilantly so as to preserve your baptismal innocence.

St. Thomas Becket

December 29

God speaks to us

The good shepherd giveth his life for his sheep.
—John 10:11

Meditation

Many difficulties encountered by the leaders of the Church come from conflicts of authority with secular rulers. One obvious example is that of St. Thomas Becket, a genuine pearl of England in the twelfth century (1117-1170). A man of duty, he did not hesitate to oppose the King in order to defend the rights of the Church while risking his own life.

His father Gilbert Becket married Matilda, the daughter of a Muslim prince, who had converted to Catholicism. Thomas was born in London in 1117, on the feast day of his patron saint. He attended the lectures of Gratian in Bologna and completed his studies in Auxerre. Theobald, Archbishop of Canterbury, had sent Thomas there because he predicted that the young man would have a bright future. Henry II Plantagenet chose him as his Chancellor. Thomas proved to be a skillful, vigorous defender of his master; in battle he showed great courage.

In 1161, when the Archbishop of Canterbury died, Thomas was called to succeed him. The King himself urged him to accept, but Thomas at first refused that office, because he knew well the pride, the jealous and greedy spirit, the haughty, vindictive irritability of Henry II. When the monarch insisted on his choice, he yielded to his entreaties.

Once he became a bishop, Thomas lived an austere life, but above all he demonstrated his acute sense of justice. He resigned from his office as Chancellor, which he deemed incompatible with that of the episcopacy. So he fell into disfavor with the violent monarch. The King took advantage of these circumstances to impose the custom whereby clerics who had been found guilty would be immediately dismissed from their offices and turned over to the secular authorities, instead of being judged by the ecclesiastical tribunals. Thomas vehemently rejected this measure, which was contrary to the rights of the Church. In revenge, the King deprived him of one of his richest castles.

Abandoned by the bishops of England, Thomas was soon forced to take refuge in France. The Pope supported him, but after he had spent two years at the Cistercian Abbey in Pontigny (the second daughter-house of Cîteaux), the King called him back to England. Thomas knew that he would meet death there, but he faced up to his duty. He took possession of his local Church again for a few weeks. On Christmas Day, he announced his impending death to the faithful, and four days late four men came to the church where he was praying and put him to death, piercing his body with a thrust of the sword.

Prayer

O God, for the sake of Whose Church the glorious Bishop Thomas fell by the sword of wicked men, grant, we beseech Thee, that all who implore his aid may obtain the good fruit of their petition. Through Jesus Christ our Lord. (Collect)

Thoughts

- "Let no one harbor the illusion of thinking that he will distinguish himself in great matters unless he first distinguishes himself in humble matters."
  —St. Francis Xavier, *PPJ*, October 14

- "No one becomes perfect all at once; along the way of goodness you begin with very little acts, so as to arrive at great ones."
  —St. Gregory the Great, *PPJ*, October 3

Resolutions

1. Recite a decade of the Rosary asking God to raise up bishops of the caliber of St. Thomas so as to extend His reign.
2. Never resort to lying.
3. Be faithful to your duty to the end, starting with the little things (punctuality, orderliness, availability).

Blessed Alain de Solminihac

December 30

GOD SPEAKS TO US

Be you therefore perfect, as also your heavenly Father is perfect.

—Matthew 5:48

MEDITATION

Originally from the province of Périgord, Alain de Solminihac (1593-1659) was blessed to be born into a noble family that was respectable both by their piety and by their honor. Thus he was in a good school to acquire the Christian virtues. At first he was destined for a military career. He easily won in tournaments, but did not let himself become inebriated with success. In his efforts to remain virtuous, he was inspired by three maxims: *"Noblesse oblige!"* [Nobility has its obligations.] "Do nothing by halves." "Act with complete perfection, for the purpose of pleasing God."

Just as he was ready to turn to knighthood in the Order of Malta, his uncle, the Abbot of Chancelade, in Périgord, handed on to him his title and responsibility as Abbot of a community of canons regular. At that time, Alain was only 21 years old. After a year of novitiate, he took the three vows of poverty, chastity, and obedience so as to consecrate himself to God in the solitude of the cloister, and he took a fourth vow obliging himself in conscience "to seek the greatest glory of God in all matters that would be of some importance." He summed up his ideal as follows: "A religious is a person who, having died to the world and to self-love, lives only for the Lord Jesus Christ."[9] By his steadfastness and his example, he succeeded in restoring fervor to his community, which until then had become quite lax. The liturgical celebrations of his monastery gave off a supernatural force

---

[9] Père Chastenet, *La Vie de Mgr de Solminihac* (1663), 89.

of attraction and an impression of interior peace. The Blessed also showed condescending charity during the famine and the plague that raged in the region in 1628 and 1629.

While Richelieu was seeking individuals worthy of being elevated to the episcopate, he spied Blessed Alain and entrusted to him the Diocese of Cahors. The holy bishop went on to administer it for 21 years. Upon his arrival, he noticed in his diocese a number of irregularities and various disorders. To stop them, he started by strengthening his clergy by showing paternal solicitude for them. He vigilantly intensified the interior life of his priests, making them other Christs, and opened a seminary to ensure higher intellectual, moral, and supernatural standards for the sacred ministers. Another priority of his was making pastoral visits. He made the rounds of his 800 parishes nine times, uprooting abuses and safeguarding the integrity of the faith and of morality. The salutary fruits that resulted were undeniable. And so, before dying, he could congratulate himself on having "re-established all things in Christ" (Eph. 1:10) and renewed his diocese.

Prayer

Grant, O almighty God, that the holy solemnity of Blessed Alain, Thy confessor and bishop, may increase devotion and salvation among us. Through Jesus Christ our Lord. (Collect)

Thoughts

- "I will work with all my might to advance in spiritual perfection."

    —Bl. Alain, *LP*, 1928

- "Nothing should be considered small in the practice of virtue."

    —Bl. Alain, *LP*, 1928

Resolutions

1 Recite the Third Joyful Mystery, asking for the spirit of poverty.
2 Seek to practice the virtue that you most lack.
3 Be helpful within the family.

St. Sylvester

December 31

GOD SPEAKS TO US

All kings of the earth shall adore Him: all nations shall serve Him.

—Psalm 71:11

MEDITATION

Born in Rome, Sylvester (+335) was a man of great intellect, great courage, and great faith. At the age of 30 he was ordained a priest by Pope St. Marcellinus. He rejoiced at the time of the Edict of Milan, which was the product of the skillful policies of Pope St. Miltiades (311-314), who advised the young Emperor Constantine and invited him to come into the Church. The latter received a nudge from heaven before a decisive battle that pitted him against Maxentius, for he discerned over the sun a luminous cross with these words: "In this sign you shall be victorious." In fact, Maxentius was defeated and drowned in the Tiber. However, after an initial period of freedom granted to the Christians, they once again had to go underground, and Sylvester himself, who had become Pope, withdrew to the harsh solitude of Mount Soracte.

Fortunately, the emperor's wavering lasted only a few months. Soon he was overcome with remorse and afflicted with a sort of leprosy. He thought then of embracing the Catholic religion, but some of his counselors tried to dissuade him by pointing out to him the risks that the empire would run if it changed its religion. He was content to reply that a religion that was capable not only of surviving but even of growing in the midst of so many persecutions can only be divine. A short time later, one night, he saw in a dream two figures who ordered him to summon the Pope, who was still hidden in Soracte. "Through baptism," they told him, "Sylvester will deliver you from the twofold leprosy of soul and body." When the Pope arrived in the emperor's presence, he expected the worst, but he was quickly reassured by the ruler's benevolent smile. When he learned of his good dispositions, he invited him to make a seven-day retreat, then baptized him and, at that very instant, Constantine completely recovered his health.

The emperor then called together a multitude of philosophers and magistrates. In their presence he pronounced a fine act of faith and promised to erect a church at the Lateran in honor of the Catholic religion. On the fourth day after his Baptism, he gave the Pope the title of Judge/King subject to his empire and, five years later (329), he handed over his Lateran Palace to the Holy Apostles Peter and Paul, and through them to Sylvester. We also owe to this holy Pope the convocation in Nicaea of the First Ecumenical Council, which promulgated the Creed to counteract the Arians who denied the divinity of Jesus Christ.

After reigning for 22 years, he could take solace in the fact that the Church that he had known when it was obscure and persecuted had become glorious and free.

Prayer

O eternal Shepherd, look favorably upon Thy flock and guard it under Thy continual protection through Blessed Sylvester, Thy Supreme Pontiff, whom Thou madest the chief shepherd of the whole Church. Through our Lord Jesus Christ. (Collect)

Thoughts

- "Faith opens the door to all the virtues."
  —St. Gregory the Great, *PPJ*, December 3

- "For each one of His elect, to walk in the presence of the Christ is to consider oneself constantly under the watchful eye of the Redeemer and to carry out what we know is pleasing to Him."
  —St. Gregory the Great, *PPJ*, December 23

Resolutions

1 Recite or sing the *Te Deum* in thanksgiving for the graces received over the course of the past year.

2 Recite the Creed. (See appendix.)

3 Defend the Catholic religion when the opportunity arises.

Holy Resolutions

January 1

GOD SPEAKS TO US

God chose us in Him before the foundation of the world, that we should be holy.

—Ephesians 1:4

MEDITATION

We are at the dawn of a new year. What does it hold in store for us? Humanly speaking, we have many reasons to be uneasy about the fate of our country and of our poor world. That is the consequence of our unfaithfulness to God. But God is always close to us to draw us to Himself, and allows us to follow in the footsteps of the saints and advance in charity toward heaven.

The saints carry out God's plan perfectly. In order to do this, they live in the present: it is up to us to imitate them. For God, there is neither past nor future. Consequently, union with Him presupposes living the present moment fully. Indeed, the past does not belong to us any more; the future does not yet belong to us; all that we have in our hands is the present moment. It is a matter of seizing this moment, marking it with the seal of grace, so as to make our actions meritorious for eternal life.

In short, human beings rarely live in the present moment. What a shame! For many temptations come through the imagination. The devil can very easily magnify past and future events so as to make us feel desires, aversion, fear, or other negative feelings. The only remedy is to live the present moment well. There is a time for everything: the success of our life depends not on our dreams, imagination, or illusions, but on virtues that we strive to acquire right where the Good Lord has put us.

The more we follow the example of the saints and submit our emotions to our will, so as to live according to the lights of the Faith, the stronger and more steadfast we will be.

In the midst of this unstable, pleasure-loving world run amok, I beg you, O saints in heaven, to accompany me throughout this year, and to help me to seek above all else the kingdom of God and His justice, so that I may sing with you eternally the mercies of the Lord.

Prayer

O my God, I thank Thee for the new year that Thou openest before me.... Holy Child, grant that I may be born to a new life.

—St. Alphonsus Liguori, *SJJ*, 17-18

Or

O my dear, sweet Savior, You decided to merit this fullness of life and of grace that is sanctity not only for a few privileged souls, but for me too.

—Père Gabriel, *ID*, 1:27

Thoughts

- "Seek ye first the kingdom of God and His justice: and all these things shall be added unto you."

  —Matthew 6:33

- "The Good Lord could not inspire unrealizable desires, therefore despite my littleness I can aspire to sanctity."
  —St. Thérèse of the Child Jesus, *PPJ*, January 3

Resolutions

1 Sing or recite the *Veni Creator*. (See appendix.)

2 Live the present moment well.

3 Put into action the virtue that you most lack.

The Holy Name of Jesus

January 2

GOD SPEAKS TO US

In the name of Jesus every knee should bow, of those that are in heaven, on earth, and under the earth, and every tongue should confess that the Lord Jesus Christ is in the glory of God the Father.

—Philippians 2:10

MEDITATION

As we go through the prophecies of the Old Testament, we discover several names that would be suitable for the Incarnate Word. Thus, the prophet Isaias had announced the mystery of the Incarnation in these terms: "Behold a virgin shall conceive and bear a son: and his name shall be called Emmanuel" (Is. 7:14). Emmanuel would go well as a term to designate the Incarnate Word because this name means "God with us." Elsewhere, Isaias also says: "A CHILD IS BORN to us, ... and his name shall be called, Wonderful, Counselor, God the Mighty, the Father of the world to come" (Is. 9:6). Jesus Christ is the wonderful God, the Prince of peace. He comes to reconcile us with His Father through His death on the cross; and He will exercise fatherhood through His authority over the souls that submit to Him.

If we leave Isaias and consult the prophet Zacharias, it would seem that the suitable name to be given to Jesus is that of "Orient" (Zach. 6:12). Indeed, Jesus is the sun of justice who comes from the East to shine in our darkness and to enlighten souls of good will.

Therefore, we have an embarrassment of riches from which to choose an adequate name for the long-awaited Messias. But in order to choose the best one, it is a good idea to ask ourselves: "What is the one that contains all the others and includes all the aspects of Christ's mission?" The Archangel Gabriel provided us with the answer on the day of the Annunciation: "Thou shalt bring forth a Son; and thou shalt call His name Jesus" (Lk. 1:31). The angel who appeared to Joseph to reveal to him the divine origin of the child confirmed it: Mary "shall bring forth a Son; and thou shalt call His name Jesus," he explained, "for He shall save His people from their sins" (Mt. 1:21). Therefore, the name best suited to Our Lord is the name of JESUS which means SAVIOR, because it is the name that designates the entirety of His mission here below.

A name in Sacred Scripture corresponds to the very nature of the person or of the thing designated thereby. For example, Our Lord changes Simon's name to Peter, because he is called to become the foundation stone of the Church (Jn. 1:42). Thus, the name of Jesus given to Our Lord corresponds perfectly to the mission that He came to carry out on earth, because He came down from heaven to save us.

Prayer

O God, Thou hast established Thine Only-begotten Son as the Savior of mankind and didst command that He should be called Jesus; mercifully grant that we who venerate His Holy Name on earth, may also be filled with the enjoyment of the vision of Him in heaven. Through the same Jesus Christ. (Collect)

Thoughts

- "All whatsoever you do in word or in work, do all in the name of the Lord Jesus Christ, giving thanks to God the Father by Him."

    —Colossians 3:17

- "Our Lord is called Prince of peace, and consequently, wherever He is the absolute master, He keeps everything in peace."

    —St. Francis de Sales, *PPJ*, January 2

Resolutions

1 Pronounce the name of Jesus only with respect.
2 Invoke the name of Jesus especially in sadness, difficulties, and temptations.
3 Become aware of the mission that you have to accomplish here on earth. However modest it may be, it is precious in God's sight.

St. Genevieve

January 3

GOD SPEAKS TO US

It is good for me to adhere to my God, to put my hope in the Lord God.

—Alleluia: Psalm 72:28

MEDITATION

God chooses what is weak in the world's estimation in order to confound the proud. He would make use of St. Genevieve (*ca.* 420-500), a simple young woman, to relieve bodies and souls, and to avert the most diabolical scourges. A native of Nanterre, Genevieve received the veil of virgins at around the age of 14 from the hands of St. Germain of Auxerre. She received the gift of healing, so that people came from all around to beg her assistance to relieve those who were overwhelmed by sickness. After her death, many sick people regained their health while praying at her tomb. But she was not content to heal bodies. She also liberated souls by her advice and her exhortations. How many souls came back to God after visiting her! And above all, she intervened miraculously at the time of the ravages caused by the Huns, led by Attila. Followed by a large army, he had already poured out his wrath on Germany, and soon the scourge would reach France.

How could his onslaught be stopped? How could he be brought back to his senses? By diplomacy? But he proudly resisted all concessions. By force? But nothing could withstand his attacks. And yet, the hour had come when he would capitulate, the hour had arrived for that cruel tyrant to lay down his weapons. A few tears shed by St. Genevieve at the foot of the altar were enough to achieve that.

Today the world might need another St. Genevieve to restore order in our country and in the Church. Nowadays only a miraculous intervention can enlighten the minds darkened by the powers of evil. It is up to everyone to prepare for this return to the Faith, to the order willed by God, by imitating the virtues practiced by St. Genevieve wherever the Good Lord has placed us.

St. Genevieve, keep me on the right path for my whole life, and give me a winning soul, a generous soul that, aware of its weakness, relies on the strength of our Lord to extend His reign in souls.

Intercession and patronage

St. Genevieve is invoked against fever, nausea, contagious diseases, and for important matters. She is the patroness of Paris, shepherd girls, and policemen.

Prayer

St. Genevieve, so loved by Jesus Christ, pray for us.
—Litany of St. Genevieve

Or

Remember, O glorious St. Genevieve, your acts of kindness to France in days of yore…. We confidently commend into your hands our spiritual and temporal interests.
—Prayer, *PS* 1:124

Thoughts

- "Seek only the glory of God and His will."
 —St. Bernadette, *PPJ*, October 17

- "Jesus must reign in my heart, in my mind, in my will, and finally in my whole soul."
 —St. Bernadette, *PPJ*, January 5

Resolutions

1 Pray to God to raise up a Catholic leader to head our country with the same enthusiasm as St. Genevieve.

2 Call on St. Genevieve several times during the day.

3 Remind others about the Catholic origins of France [and of many regions of the United States and Canada] the next time the opportunity arises.

St. Angela of Foligno

January 4

GOD SPEAKS TO US

I came not to call the just, but sinners.

—Mark 2:17

MEDITATION

Angela was born in Foligno in Umbria near Assisi (Italy). Married at the age of 20, she had several children. During the first years of her marriage, she did not take seriously her mission as wife or mother, leading instead a frivolous, worldly life. Nevertheless the grace of God was at work in her soul, and finally she decided to be reconciled with Him. She went to confession, but unfortunately she did not dare to admit everything to her confessor, and despite this she went to receive the Sacred Host, thus making a sacrilegious communion. At that moment, St. Francis of Assisi appeared to her to rebuke her for her conduct. She then changed completely, devoted herself to prayer, and led a very mortified life after distributing her goods to the poor. The people around her thought she had gone mad. At that time she lost her mother, her husband, and her children, one right after the other.

She then entered the Third Order Franciscans. Very quickly she was raised to a high degree of perfection and was favored with visions of Our Lord suffering. The Passion of Jesus was, indeed, the principal object of her contemplation. One Holy Thursday she heard Jesus tell her distinctly: "I did not love you as a joke."[10] She understood instantly how very weak and languid her own love for Christ was in comparison to Jesus' love for her.

Besides meditating on the Passion, she particularly loved to pray the Our Father. She recited it often, but she understood that these prayers and meditations would remain fruitless without the practice of humility. In this area, the

---

[10] St. Angela of Foligno, *Book of Revelations*, chap. 33.

saints are often more admirable than imitable. Indeed, overcoming her repugnance, one day she drank the water that she had used to wash the feet of a leper. She wanted to treat this leper like Jesus Himself, and to compensate him for his abandonment by other people. She died very peacefully at the age of 61 on January 4, 1309, after having spoken on the previous day the words of Jesus: "Father, into Thy hands I commend my spirit."

St. Angela, by your life you teach me that it is never too late to do good. The present hour can redeem my past miseries. Thus, help me to follow you along the path of virtue through the practice of humility and the loving contemplation of the Passion of Jesus.

Prayer

God, sweetness of hearts and light of the blessed, Who didst allow Thy servant Angela to enjoy an admirable contemplation of heavenly things, grant that by her merits and intercession we may know Thee here on earth, so that we might merit to enjoy in heaven the vision of Thy eternal glory. (Collect)

Thoughts

- "May your thoughts be always fixed on the things of heaven and ceaselessly cherish the memory of Jesus crucified, Who wants you to reproduce His life by the practice of penance and the holiness of your works."
—St. Angela, *Au. S.*, 1:749

- "Let us generously climb the slopes of Calvary for love of Him who Was sacrificed for love of us."
—Padre Pio, *ASN,* 42

Resolutions

1. Recite the litany of humility. (See appendix.)
2. Allow sufficient time for your examination of conscience.
3. Pray to the Blessed Virgin, for example, the *Memorare*, before your examination of conscience so as to conceal nothing in confession. (See appendix.)

St. Simeon Stylites

January 5

GOD SPEAKS TO US

Blessed are they that mourn.... Blessed are the clean of heart.

—Matthew 5:5, 8

MEDITATION

St. Simeon was born in Cilicia (Turkey) at the end of the fourth century. He was a shepherd. After hearing the Gospel passage about the Beatitudes during a Mass, he asked an old man how he could reach this happiness. The man replied: "You can attain it by prayer, fasting, and humility." Simeon had the idea of joining one of his cousins, who was a religious. The rule of the monastery was very strict, but he far surpassed his brothers by his fervor and mortification. Simeon ate only once a week and had as his belt a cord made of palm leaves that he fastened so tight that it left a deep wound. After ten years had passed, the superior of the convent urged him to leave the monastery because his very unusual conduct could be an occasion of scandal for some brothers.

He departed for the desert and the idea occurred to him to imitate the 40-day fast of Moses and Elias. He asked permission from the superior of a nearby monastery, who granted it on the condition that he would take with him some bread and water to sustain himself in the case of extreme necessity. St. Simeon brought with him his little supply of food and drink, but he did not touch it.

Soon his reputation for sanctity was so great that a large number of believers came from all sides to see him and to beg him to grant them many favors. At his touch, the sick were healed, sinners changed their way of life, unbelievers were converted. His reputation spread to Italy, Gaul, and Great Britain, but also to Persia, Armenia, Arabia, and as far as India. Pilgrims arrived in great throngs, and the people who approached him tried to touch his habit so as to obtain the favors that they expected from him. In order to protect himself from the touches of the pilgrims, the saint had the idea of building a column 20 meters [65 feet] tall. They gave him the name *Stylites*, since *stylê* in Greek means "column." Perched up there, the saint prayed, preached to the crowds, and prophesied. He remained on his column for almost 37 years. An immeasurable crowd pressed in on him to see him. Consequently, "as the famous historian Tillemont says, his story is as certain as it is extraordinary."[11]

When death arrived in 459, the saint bowed down to pray as usual. In that posture he gave his beautiful soul back to God.

Prayer

O Lord, show me how pure my heart must be in order to be admitted to Your intimate friendship.

—Father Gabriel, *ID*, 2:51

Thoughts

- "Let us have no treasure on earth, so that our heart may not be attached to anything earthly."

    —Charles de Foucauld, *PPJ*, February 7

- "Let us strive with all our might to make sure that our mind is always occupied with God or with what He orders us to do in His service."

    —Charles de Foucauld, *PPJ*, January 29

Reflections

1 Avoid the systematic search for comfort, and accept discomforts in a spirit of penance.

2 Make an effort to place yourself correctly in the presence of God when you pray and to assume a posture worthy of it.

3 Do not complain about the weather.

---

[11] Abbé Dunand, *Histoires choisies des Pères de déserts d'Orient* (Édouard Privat, 1894), 203.

Epiphany – The Three Kings

January 6

GOD SPEAKS TO US

We have seen His star in the East and have come to adore Him.

—Matthew 2:2

MEDITATION

Tradition has preserved the names of the Magi, or Three Kings: Melchior, Casper (Gaspard), and Balthasar. The first represented the race of Sem, the second—the race of Cham, and the third—the race of Japheth [see Gen. 10:1]. As descendants of the sons of Noe, those three men gathered in themselves the whole human race that Jesus came to save. Their expedition from the East to Bethlehem reveals their generosity. The discovered a mysterious star. The Holy Ghost, enlightening them interiorly, made them understand that it was the announcement of the birth of the Messias and that it was to serve as their guide enabling them to travel to Him and adore Him. Immediately, without waiting for additional explanations, they left their houses, their families, their native lands. They did not know how much time their journey would take nor what obstacles they would have to overcome. God had spoken; that was enough, and they obeyed. Let us imitate their promptness when the Holy Ghost shows us a sacrifice to make, an act of charity to perform, a disorderly attachment to break; let us not weigh up our efforts, let us be generous. We should form the habit of seizing grace when it comes by.

It was still relatively easy for the Magi to follow the star, but for them to continue to seek the King of the Jews when it had disappeared was the mark of a great spirit of faith. In the midst of their trial, they were not scandalized, they did not rebel, they did not call their faith into question; they bowed

Epiphany – The Three Kings

in silence before the mysterious designs of Providence. Its ways are not our ways, they told each other. And so they redoubled their generosity and fervor so as to stay the course on which they had set out. If sometimes in our life God is hidden when we pray to Him, let us imitate the Magi. We, too, demonstrate the firmness of our faith by keeping our convictions and remaining faithful to our resolutions.

Following the instructions of the scholars of the Law, the Magi had the extraordinary grace of contemplating Jesus. After a trial comes the reward. The faith that they demonstrated when they departed on their expedition—and even more when the star disappeared—found its crowning, completion, and reward at the manger. By entering into the humble stable in Bethlehem, they saw with their own eyes the infant Jesus in swaddling clothes, flanked by His mother and St. Joseph. Going beyond His mortal wrappings, their faith discovered God in that infant, so that they fell prostrate and adored Him.

Prayer

O God, on this day, by the guiding star, Thou didst reveal Thine Only-begotten Son to the Gentiles; mercifully grant, that we who now know Thee by faith, may be led on to behold the beauty of Thy Majesty. (Collect)

Thoughts

- "The homages and the adoration of the Three Kings kneeling at the manger were lifted up to Jesus through the hands and through the heart of Mary. May it be the same with my adoration, Most Blessed Virgin."
  —Charles de Foucauld, *PPJ*, February 7

- "The Magi advanced, following the star they had seen, which went before them; its light led them to the Light, and they professed a God by their gifts."
  —Hymn at Vespers

Resolutions

1. Imitate the promptness of the Magi by arising the first time the alarm clock sounds.
2. Do not neglect to pray to Our Lady of the way when you travel, and call on St. Raphael and your guardian angel.
3. Practice holy resignation when faced with a thankless task at work or at home.

The Holy Family

The Sunday after January 6

GOD SPEAKS TO US

The parents of Jesus carried Him to Jerusalem, to present Him to the Lord.

—Offertory: Luke 2:22

MEDITATION

Knowing that we need examples in order to make progress in life, God willed to give us in the Holy Family an unsurpassable, admirable model that can be imitated to a great extent. What is striking on first glance is that everyone in it is at his place. St. Joseph, spouse of Our Lady and foster father of Jesus, fulfills his duties as husband and father for the best. He is conscious of his mission as head of the family, and in no way does he shirk his obligations, which were sometimes very burdensome. Recall the particularly painful circumstances of the birth of Jesus: having to go door to door to find a house that might welcome them, being rejected everywhere, and resigning himself to take shelter in a poor stable. Shortly after the Infant's birth, an angel awakened him in the middle of the night and told him to take the Child and His Mother and to flee to Egypt. What a trial for him and for Our Lady to leave like that for a foreign country without knowing where they could settle or for how long. St. Joseph does not argue about the angel's orders, any more than Our Lady questions those of her husband. The harmony of the household comes from the fact that each one carries out his duty the best he can and, instead of making the others' duties more difficult, facilitates them by his profound and complete support.

As for Mary, she is the heart of the home. Sacred Scripture shows her to us as a contemplative woman and at the same time as very active. Far from being turned in on herself, she lives a life that is open to others. After the Annunciation, she travels in haste to visit her cousin Elizabeth, who is pregnant with St. John the Baptist. In Cana, she notices the lack of wine and the embarrassment that this will cause the organizers of the wedding feast. She seeks to please others so as to make life more agreeable around her. The mutual support of St. Joseph and Our Lady moderated their trials.

Their zeal was increased tenfold by the fine example of the Divine Child. St. Luke sums up Jesus' attitude during His hidden life in these words: "He was subject to them" (Lk. 2:51). Obedience is the holiness of children. Docility makes characters more flexible and enables them to accept trials better.

Let us take the Holy Family, then, as our model. Life on earth can be a hell, a purgatory, or to some extent an anticipation of heaven. It depends in large part on our conduct within our family, on how we react to trials, on our way of looking at the events in life. And so it is up to each of us to ask himself what he can do to make his family life come ever closer to the life of the saints in heaven.

Prayer

O Lord Jesus Christ, by subjecting Thyself to Mary and Joseph, Thou didst consecrate family life with wonderful virtues; grant that, by their joint assistance, we may fashion our lives after the example of Thy Holy Family and obtain everlasting fellowship with it. (Collect)

Thoughts

- "Do not upset one another in this home where you have so many reasons to be lenient toward one another."
  —Msgr. Chevrot, *VF*, p. 34
- "Let us listen patiently to those who confide in us."
  —Msgr. Chevrot, *VF*, p. 51

Resolutions

1 Patiently accept the contradictions of the day.
2 Show gentleness within the family by your smile.
3 In the family, encourage one another mutually and take the opportunities to show gratitude to your close friends and relatives.

Jesus, Model of Poverty

January 8

GOD SPEAKS TO US

They found Mary and Joseph, and the Infant lying in the manger.

—Luke 2:16

MEDITATION

Today and for the next few days we will meditate on several virtues of the Child Jesus that the saints were able to admire and reproduce in their lives. Jesus did not come to earth to make a tourist trip; He did not come to lead a life of pleasure; He came in painful, disastrous, tragic circumstances. His descent to earth is connected with very disappointing circumstances. Man did not remain faithful to the law given to him. He preferred to listen to the devil's voice than to the voice of his God. He defied God's law and by that very fact sullied himself and made himself the devil's slave. In separating himself from God, he contracted a threefold wound: a disordered attachment to his own will, another to the pleasures of life, and a third to the goods of this world. In order to teach him detachment from material goods, Jesus chose to be born in a stable.

But another reason guided Our Lord in His choice. If the angels had said to the shepherds: "The Savior is born in the most beautiful house in the village, at the synagogue leader's home. His parents are illustrious descendants of King David…," this altogether human magnificence would have dampened their enthusiasm. "Good for Him," they would have thought, "the Savior is born, but with our tattered clothing and dirty hands, we cannot decently appear before Him." And a slight sadness would have clouded their joy. Fortunately, the angel said to them: "And this shall be a sign unto you. You shall find the Infant wrapped in swaddling clothes and laid in a manger" (Lk. 2:12).

Upon hearing this message, the shepherds were quite moved. Instead of the linen robe of little Samuel, the Infant

Jesus was clothed with diapers, scraps of cloth. A manger for cattle held Him instead of a cradle. The Savior of mankind rested on a little straw, less fortunate than the newborn of a shepherd.

Well, then, the shepherds did not hesitate for an instant. They said to one another: "Let us go over to Bethlehem and let us see this word that is come to pass" (Lk. 2:15). Notice that they already were speaking the language of faith. This little insignificant incident—a baby who was brought into the world amid the hazards of traveling, in a makeshift shelter—was for them something great, a very great thing, the greatest.

As they arrived at the manger, full of wonder, they met the gentle, pleasant, kind glance of the Infant Jesus, who lay between an ox and an ass, watched over by His virginal Mother and good St. Joseph!

Prayer

Grant, we beseech Thee, Almighty God, that the new birth of Thine Only-begotten Son as man may set us free, who are held by the old bondage under the yoke of sin. Through the same Jesus Christ. (Collect for Christmas, Mass during the Day)

Thoughts

- "The Infant Jesus in His swaddling clothes preferred humility instead of the great glory and ardor of His angels."
  —St. Thérèse of the Child Jesus, *PPJ*, December 22

- "O my dear Mother, how kind and great you seem to me in such a poor place!"
  —St. Thérèse of the Child Jesus, *PPJ*, December 24

JESUS, MODEL OF POVERTY

RESOLUTIONS

1 Recite the Third Joyful Mystery to obtain the grace to face monetary worries with the spirit of Jesus in the manger.

2 Accept the loss of an object, or let it be taken away if it is not indispensable, in the spirit of poverty.

3 Lend your things willingly to someone who requests it.

Jesus, Model of Charity

January 9

GOD SPEAKS TO US

A light shall shine upon us this day: for the Lord is born to us.

—Introit, Mass at Dawn, Isaias 9:2, 6

MEDITATION

The saints imitated Jesus so as to attain perfection. Following their example, let us strive to learn lessons from the manger.

In the stable in Bethlehem, Jesus manifested not only His spirit of poverty, but also His charity. In seeing the newborn, a skeptic would have said, "one more poor person"; but because the eyes of their heart were simple, the shepherds understood that it would be possible for the weak and the poor to be saved by Jesus, who was little, weak, and poor like them, and that He already felt the suffering of mankind in His flesh, before experiencing it in His heart. In His presence, no human being can say: "He is not for me." He is absolutely one of us. Although unable to explain it clearly, the shepherds sensed that Christmas reveals to mankind the nature of true greatness. From now on the great will no longer be those who are served, but those who serve. Greatness is service, bearing the burdens of others, showing mercy. What they glimpsed, we Catholics know: God wants to save all human beings because He loves them all. Someone may pretend not to know this and another may strive to deny it. No one, however, will prevent Him from seeking to save us as long as we are on earth.

Jesus is happy to have become man so as to teach us our noble task as human beings, which is to pray, work, suffer, love God above all else, and love one another for the love of God. He comes to restore to us our greatness, which had been debased by sin, to give us the power to become children of God, and in order to do that He will die as He is born, in solitude, in suffering, and in utter poverty.

The shepherds in Bethlehem could not know what we know. Nevertheless, St. Luke declares that they "returned, glorifying and praising God for all the things they had heard and seen" (Lk. 2:20). After that unique moment, they returned to their flocks; they continued to sleep on the ground, eat very simple food, and be on the lowest rung of society. Nothing changed in their living conditions, but everything changed in their life after they had seen Jesus make Himself little like them and choose an existence similar to theirs. From then on they knew that God loved them, since He had called them to celebrate the birth of His. They heard the angels singing that God, who reigns in heaven, giving to the earth the gift of His dearly-beloved Son.

Prayer

Grant us, we beseech Thee, almighty God, that we on whom the new light of Thine Incarnate Word is poured, may show forth in our works that brightness, which now illuminates our minds by faith. Through the same Jesus Christ. (Collect for Christmas, Mass at Dawn)

Thoughts

- "Where does holiness dwell, if not in the Christian who is at the disposal of everyone, always willing to render service?"

    —Msgr. Chevrot, *VF*, p. 51

- "Let us be infinitely delicate in our charity. Let us not limit ourselves to major services; let us have that delicate tact that enters into the details and by means of seemingly insignificant things can bring so much comfort to hearts."

    —Charles de Foucauld, *PPJ*, September 30

Resolutions

1. Pray the Act of Charity. (See appendix.)
2. Forgive those who have hurt us the most and recite a decade of the Rosary for their salvation.
3. Render a service to your neighbor and offer it for the intention of pleasing God.

Jesus, Model of Purity

January 10

GOD SPEAKS TO US

Blessed are the clean of heart, for they shall see God.
—Matthew 5:8

MEDITATION

Ever since He came into this world, Jesus taught us not only to be charitable and detached from the goods of this world, but also to be pure. St. Leo, in a reading from the Office of Matins for Christmas Day, declares that "What is said about all men: 'No one is pure from stain, not even a child who has lived only one day on earth,' cannot be applied to this nativity. We find no concupiscence of the flesh in this miraculous birth; nothing proceeding from the law of sin. A virgin was chosen from the house of David: a royal virgin destined to carry the sacred offspring in her womb, who conceived the Man-God spiritually by faith before conceiving Him in a bodily way."[12] The Infant Jesus is free from all stain, and His Mother is the most-pure Virgin, while St. Joseph is the protector of virgins.

The virtues are interconnected; in other words, they call for each other. Thus charity presupposes purity and nourishes it. Indeed, the Good Lord gave us a heart to love Him with a deep love, an unselfish love, a preferential love. God's first commandment is to love God with our whole heart, with our whole strength, and with our whole mind, and the second is to love our neighbor as ourselves. This twofold love is not that easy to put into practice because of the aftereffects left in us by original sin. Our ability to love is disordered.

According to Aristotle, there are two forms of human love: a love of concupiscence and a love of benevolence. In the love of concupiscence, the person takes a creature and refers it exclusively to himself because it is pleasing or useful

---

[12] St. Leo, Matins for Christmas Day, Fifth Reading.

to him. For example, I love chocolate because of the pleasure that I experience in eating it. I value my automobile because of the convenience that this means of transportation offers me. But in a human being there is another form of love in which the person no longer takes but gives of himself. This is called the "love of benevolence." It consists of desiring the good of the beloved persons and doing good for them. Both forms of love are beneficial, but it is important above all to develop the second, because a human being is made, not primarily to take, but rather to give, to give himself. Jesus teaches this from His cradle onward.

O Jesus, give me the grace to practice the beautiful virtue of purity, following the example of the saints, by loving my neighbor with a generous, unselfish love.

Prayer

St. Joseph, grant that, preserved from all stain, with a pure mind and heart, and with a chaste body, I may constantly serve Jesus and Mary in perfect purity.

—Prayer to obtain purity

Thoughts

- "The purer the heart, and the more detached it is from visible things, the more divine love interiorly touches, arouses, and inflames it."

    —Bourdalou, *OEC*, IV, p. 593

- "How can a heart addicted to affection for creatures be closely united to God? ... I think that that is not possible."

    —St. Thérèse of the Child Jesus, *PC*, p. 173

Resolutions

1 Never voluntarily keep looking at an indecent image.

2 Avoid unhealthy daydreaming at all costs.

3 Turn to God immediately in temptations.

Jesus, Model of Obedience

January 11

GOD SPEAKS TO US

[Jesus] was subject to them.

—Luke 2:51

MEDITATION

From the moment of His Incarnation, Jesus showed His obedience by stating: "Behold, I come to do Thy will, O God" (Heb. 10:7). Until His death He would remain faithful to His promise, to the point where He would say in all truth on Holy Thursday evening in His prayer to His Father: "I have finished the work that Thou gavest Me to do" (Jn. 17:4) and finally, before breathing His last, He would utter these triumphant words: "It is consummated" (Jn. 19:30), which means: "I have perfectly accomplished the mission that You entrusted to Me."

Jesus is a model for us. He tells His apostles clearly: "Not every one that saith to Me, Lord, Lord, shall enter into the kingdom of heaven: but he that doth the will of My Father who is in heaven, he shall enter into the kingdom of heaven" (Mt. 7:21). The saints who take His teaching to heart imitate Him in His obedience. This virtue is often difficult for us because it obliges us to sacrifice the thing we are most attached to, namely our own will. Through obedience, we submit our will to the will of our superior. Now, of all goods, the most precious are those of the soul; chief among these is the will, since we make use of the other goods through it.

The difficulty is increased by the aftereffects left in us by original sin. Since the offence of our first parents was a sin of disobedience, we are weakened in this respect. It is difficult for our will to submit to those who have authority over us because, spontaneously, we prefer to do what pleases us instead of our duty. We do not like to be corrected or counseled, even for our good; we aspire to ever-greater independence, to more and more freedom.

While emphasizing the importance of obedience, we must not forget that it is a moral virtue and, as such, it is situated at a happy medium. Although it too often happens that we chafe at the yoke of authority out of a spirit of independence, it can also happen that we submit unduly to an authority when it imposes on us something against faith or morality. In those circumstances, we must imitate St. Peter, who said: "We ought to obey God rather than men" (Acts 5:29).

O saints of heaven, intercede for me with God so that my will may be more flexible and I might imitate you in the practice of obedience!

Prayer

Help me, my God, to go beyond all the human aspects of obedience, so as to come into contact with You and with Your divine will.

—Father Gabriel, *ID*, vol. II, p. 185

Thoughts

- "Obedience is the key that opened the door which had been closed by Adam's disobedience."

    —St. Catherine of Siena, *D*, vol. II, p. 252.

- "Where there is no obedience, there is no virtue. Where there is no virtue, there is no love. Where there is no love, God is not present. And without God, no one goes to paradise."

    —Padre Pio, *PPJ*, July 14

Resolutions

1 Recite a decade of the Rosary for your superiors.

2 Be content with the place assigned to you in your family, in your workplace, whatever it might be, and in order to do that, look at it as a gift from the Good Lord.

3 Be on time to your appointments.

Jesus, Source of Joy

January 12

GOD SPEAKS TO US

Rejoice in the Lord always: again, I say, rejoice.
—Philippians 4:4

MEDITATION

If we look superficially at the sacrifices that a good Christian life involves, we may wonder how the saints, endowed with the same human nature as we, were capable of so much renunciation. The only explanation for this is the intensity of their love for God. The lives of the saints are ultimately a love story. St. Thomas Aquinas explains that "every man loves what is beautiful: carnal men love carnal beauty, and spiritual men love spiritual beauty."[13] Loving God with their whole heart, the saints experienced extraordinary spiritual joys that multiplied their fervor and generosity tenfold, since God is the source of joy.

On major liturgical feast days, God puts into generous, fervent hearts feelings of love and gratitude that fill them with joy. As St. Leo said in celebrating the Feast of Christmas, "Dearly beloved, our Savior was born today: let us rejoice. There must be no sadness on the day on which Life is born, the life which dispels the fear of death and thus spreads joy in our souls through the promise of eternity. There is no one who does not share in this gladness. All have the same reason to rejoice, because when Our Lord, the destroyer of sin and death, found us all subject to sin, He came to liberate us. Let him who is holy thrill, because he is about to win the palm. Let the sinner rejoice, because here he is being invited to forgiveness. May the pagan take courage, because he is invited to life."[14] St. Leo renews his call to rejoice on the liturgical day of Epiphany because, he

---

[13] St. Thomas Aquinas, *Commentaire sur les psaumes* (Paris: Cerf, 1996), 311.
[14] St. Leo, Christmas Matins, Fourth Reading.

says, "shortly after the Solemnity of the Nativity of Jesus Christ, the feast of His manifestation resounds in turn."[15]

Fortified by these celebrations, O Jesus, I want to spend the season of Epiphany in joy, and to imitate the saints in their renunciation, so as to taste fully the delicious fruits of the beatitudes, the first-fruits of the happiness that You have prepared for us in the blessed eternity of heaven.

Prayer

Sing joyfully to God, all the earth: serve ye the Lord with gladness. Come in before His presence with exceeding great joy. Know ye that the Lord he is God.
—Psalm 99:2-3

Thoughts

- "The only happiness that we have on earth is to love God and to know that God loves us."
—The Curé of Ars, St. John Vianney, *PPJ2*, January 30

- "Seeing the star, they rejoiced with exceeding great joy."
—Matthew 2:10

Resolutions

1 Seek to make life pleasant and peaceful around you by avoiding arguments and treating others tactfully.

2 Keep joy in your heart by considering the graces you have received from God, so as to have a happy face which gives others the desire to be Catholics.

3 Do not be eager for news (limit your use of the internet; shut off the radios and television sets) and do not let human predictions of catastrophes affect you.

---

[15] St. Leo, Epiphany Matins, Fourth Reading.

The Baptism of Jesus

January 13

God speaks to us

"He upon whom thou shalt see the Spirit descending and remaining upon Him, He it is that baptizeth with the Holy Ghost." And I saw: and I gave testimony that this is the Son of God.

—St. John 1:33-34

Meditation

Our Lord lowered Himself to our level; this was in order to lift us up from sin and to admit us to intimate friendship with Him. Our union with Him is brought about essentially by the Sacraments. In order to grasp this, let us contemplate His baptism in the Jordan by St. John the Baptist.

At the moment when Jesus was in the water and St. John was baptizing Him, suddenly the heavens opened, a dove descended upon Our Lord, and a voice could be heard saying: "This is My beloved Son" (Mt. 3:17).

The dove symbolizes peace. Now St. Paul says that one of the fruits of the Holy Ghost is peace (Gal. 5:22). This is why the Holy Ghost appears today under this form. But above all, His presence during the baptism of Jesus announces His coming in the souls of the faithful on the day of their baptism. (*Cf.* Mt. 3:11.)

The Father's voice, declaring, "This is My beloved Son," tells us that, through baptism, we in turn have become children of God.[16]

The heavens opening show that one fruit of baptism is admission to heaven.[17] Even the place of Jesus' baptism confirms this. Indeed, the Jordan is the last river that the Hebrews crossed dry shod in order to reach the Promised Land—a prefiguration of heaven.[18]

---

[16] St. Thomas Aquinas, *Summa theologiae*, III, q. 39, art. 8.
[17] St. Thomas Aquinas, *Summa theologiae*, III, q. 39, art. 5.
[18] St. Thomas Aquinas, *Summa theologiae*, III, q. 39, art. 4.

O Jesus, thank You for the grace of my baptism. On that day, I became your child and an heir of heaven. Therefore help me always to behave in a way befitting my dignity.

Prayer

O God, Who established the nature of man in wondrous dignity, and still more admirably restored it, grant that through the mystery of this water and wine, we may be made partakers of His Divinity, Who has condescended to become partaker of our humanity. (Offertory of the Mass)
Or

O God, Whose Only-begotten Son appeared in the substance of our flesh, grant, we beseech Thee, that by Him, in Whom outwardly we recognize our likeness, we may deserve to be inwardly created anew. (Collect)

Thoughts

- "Baptism is what made you an adopted child and marked you with the seal of the Holy Trinity."
  —Elizabeth of the Trinity, *PPJ*, January 13

- "Reflect that a Being whose name is Love dwells in us at every moment of the day and night, and that He asks us to live in fellowship with Him."
  —Elizabeth of the Trinity, *PPJ*, May 30

Resolutions

1 Have your children baptized as early as possible so as to allow them to become children of God.

2 Make the sign of the cross well, remembering that we were baptized in the name of the Father, and of the Son, and of the Holy Ghost.

3 Renew every year your baptismal promises one the anniversary of the day on which you were baptized.

St. Hilary

January 14

GOD SPEAKS TO US

The mouth of the just man tells of wisdom and his tongue utters what is right.

—Gradual: Psalm 36:30

MEDITATION

Hilary was born in Aquitaine (Gaul) around the year 315. He embraced the Catholic faith only after mature reflection. He wondered about the purpose of life. Was it merely for the enjoyment of material goods? But he said to himself: human happiness must not be found in the pleasures of the senses, because human beings have this in common with animals. If that was the case, we would even be at a disadvantage in comparison to some animals, since they do not work and they eat as much as they want.

Having ruled out a purely sensory happiness, Hilary asked himself whether human happiness is found in the satisfactions of the intellect. But he realized that often those who set their final purpose in the satisfactions of the mind are proud and full of themselves. If it is true that a carnal man's god is his stomach, then the god of the self-proclaimed wise man is pride. Therefore, he pursued his search in another direction. Passing beyond material or purely intellectual happiness, he arrived at the conclusion that man would find his happiness in God and in God alone. The trials of the present life are there to make him merit a much happier, much more pleasant life in the next world.

Moreover, he said to himself that the true God could not be the one that the pagans adored. Indeed, he recognized that there can be only one God who is eternal, almighty, unchangeable, infinitely beautiful, and source of all beauty. Then he reflected that the Good Lord cannot leave the just without a reward. And so he was overjoyed to learn that God became a little child so as to let us become children of God.

Once he was baptized, he was such great pity for souls that he was chosen to become Bishop of Poitiers. He applied all his zeal in the service of the faith and had to defend the Catholic position against the Arians. For this he was exiled to Asia Minor. Then, after returning to Gaul, he drove out the serpents on the Island of Gallinaria, near Gênes, by planting his staff in the middle of the island. Once he was in Gaul, he strove to bring the rebellious bishops back to the true faith. Then, he continued his work of evangelization in Italy, with the help of St. Eusebius of Vercelli. Finally he was compelled to return to Gaul, where he died peacefully on January 13, 368.

THOUGHTS

- "To remain silent when one ought to speak is cowardice and not modesty."
  —St. Hilary, *Book against Constantius*, n. 1

- "It is better to die than to yield to the authority of a man and stain the virginity of my faith."
  —St. Hilary, *Book against Constantius*

RESOLUTIONS

1. Recite a decade of the Rosary for the bishops of your country, that they may be authentic teachers of the Faith.

2. Make use of the time when traveling (walking, using public transportation, driving) to reflect on the nature of true happiness.

3. Read a leaflet or a chapter from a book on doctrine about an article of the faith that you are not well acquainted with.

St. Paul, The First Hermit

January 15

GOD SPEAKS TO US

The just man shall flourish like the palm tree, like a cedar of Lebanon shall he grow.

—Introit: Psalm 91:13

MEDITATION

St. Paul the Hermit lived in the third and fourth centuries. During the Decian persecution, while still very young, he withdrew to the countryside with his sister and brother-in-law to wait for better days. He lost his parents at the age of 15 and found himself the owner of extensive properties. His brother-in-law, who wanted to seize them, denounced him as a Christian so that Paul fled to the mountains in the Egyptian desert of the Thebaid.

After moving from one secluded spot to another, he finally arrived at the foot of a cliff, beneath which was a cavern with an opening to the sky, over which a palm tree extended its branches. A clear stream came from the cliff and dispersed in the ground.

Paul, then 23 years old, settled down for a permanent retreat in that spot and lived a holy life there until the age of 113 (†340). St. Jerome told the story of his life, which is admirable from several perspectives. First of all, the spirit of detachment from the goods of this world. Rather than bear a grudge against his brother-in-law for having denounced him as a Christian, he preferred to flee to the desert. Thus, he demonstrated the utmost trust in Providence, and the Good Lord rewarded him for it by sending him each day his daily bread through a crow.

Moreover, he gave a very cordial welcome to St. Anthony, who came to visit him. Shortly after that meeting, Anthony saw him going up to heaven clothed with a dazzling white robe in the company of angels, prophets, and apostles. Then he went in search of the hermit's mortal remains, and found his body kneeling, with head raised and arms outstretched toward heaven. Two lions then came to dig his grave and then Anthony was able to lower his friend's body into it and cover it with earth.

Great St. Paul, I wish to live closer to God so that this close contact with my Creator and Savior may make me humbler, kinder, gentler, more courteous, and more tactful toward my neighbor. Help to acquire as you did a sense of God's majesty, grandeur, and goodness, so that I might become more charitable toward my neighbor.

Attributes

St. Paul is depicted as a hermit, wearing palm leaves and accompanied by a crow.

Prayer

O God, Thou dost gladden us by the annual feast of Blessed Paul, Thy Confessor; mercifully grant that we may imitate his example, whose heavenly birthday we celebrate. Through our Lord.... (Collect)

Thoughts

- "Let us withdraw to the desert with our Master and ask Him to teach us to live by His life."
   —Elizabeth of the Trinity, *PPJ*, July 30

- "Live in close intimacy with Him, as one lives with a beloved person, in a pleasant heart-to-heart conversation."
   —Elizabeth of the Trinity, *PPJ*, August 8

Resolutions

1 Recite the Third Joyful Mystery, asking for detachment from the goods of this world and abandonment to Divine Providence.

2 Prepare for death. For example on the next Saturday of the month, put yourself in the right dispositions of mind and heart to be ready to appear before God.

3 Avoid the sources of dissipation and distraction (radio, computer, cellphone) so as to be more closely united to God.

St. Marcellus

January 16

God speaks to us

The God of all grace, Who has called us unto His eternal glory in Christ Jesus, will Himself, after we have suffered a little while, perfect, strengthen, and establish us.

—First Epistle of St. Peter 5:10

Meditation

St. Marcellus was Pope at the end of the times of persecution, shortly before freedom was granted to the Church by the Emperor Constantine.

During the first centuries of Church history, the martyrs were the seeds of the Faith: the more martyrs there were, the more the Christian religion grew. The cross, when carried generously, is fruitful. It is the source of salvation. The saints accepted it patiently and confidently, knowing that God would bring good from it at one time or another.

St. Marcellus was Pope during the reign of the Emperor Maxentius after the great persecutions by Diocletian and Maximinian. At the beginning of his pontificate, Maxentius let the Christians live in peace because he needed them to establish his authority. But as soon as he felt sufficiently strong, he began to persecute them savagely. Pope Marcellus himself was scourged and sentenced to live for nine months in a cowshed, tending the animals that were used in the games of the city.

Set free one night by some Christians, he was welcomed by Lucina, a pious Christian woman, but his liberty was short-lived. He was arrested a second time and compelled to tend animals in the church where he was staying, which on that occasion was transformed into a stable. Finally, he died of exhaustion as a result of the terrible conditions in 309, the sixth year of his pontificate. On his mortal remains they found a hair shirt (actually in this case a rough belt made of animal hair), a sign of his extreme mortification. St. Marcellus is therefore a fine example of a Pope who was faithful in the midst of the most painful and humiliating persecutions.

St. Marcellus, the Holy Catholic Church today is to a large extent degraded by liberalism and modernism. Therefore, intercede on her behalf, that she may very quickly regain her former splendor, and pray to Jesus that all those who have a position of responsibility in the Church might be faithful to their sublime vocation.

Attributes

St. Marcellus is depicted with horses or donkeys, in the stable where he was compelled to tend them like a groom.

Prayer

O Eternal Shepherd, look favorably upon Thy flock, and guard it by Thy continual protection through Blessed Marcellus, Thy Martyr and Supreme Pontiff, whom Thou madest the chief shepherd of the whole Church. (Collect)

Thoughts

- "No saint reached heavenly glory without practicing patience."

    —St. Gregory the Great, *PPJ*, November 3

- "The holy martyrs are there, your defenders, but they want us to pray to them and, so to speak, pray that people will pray to them."

    —St. Gregory the Great, *PPJ*, November 21

Resolutions

1 Recite the Third Glorious Mystery, asking that the Pope might surround himself with prelates whose sole concern is to use their talents to be staunch promoters of Catholic doctrine and morals.

2 Ask God to raise up priestly and religious vocations and to instill missionary zeal into Catholics.

3 Make a sacrifice so that a wayward sinner may return to the faith.

St. Anthony, Abbot

January 17 (Our Lady of Pontmain: see Jan. 19)

GOD SPEAKS TO US

The mouth of the just man tells of wisdom and his tongue utters what is right. The law of his God is in his heart.
—Introit: Psalm 36:30

MEDITATION

Born in 251 in the village of Qeman in Upper Egypt, St. Anthony was a giant of holiness. At the age of 20 he sold his properties for benefit of the poor and withdrew from the world. He led a very mortified life, spending his time working and praying, sleeping very little, content with food that was more than frugal. He endured the trial of temptation, and he knew it in all its most dangerous forms. Hell received permission to torment this Christian Job and to deploy all its wiles against him. And so, how stubbornly and relentlessly it unleashed its most perfidious henchmen to make him fall! Sensuous pleasure assumed all kinds of forms, from the most seductive charms of a shameless courtesan to the most repulsive shapes of horrible animals. Day and night there were perpetual snares and attacks. Armed with grace, he stood firm as a rock in the midst of the most furious storms. He fought against the bellowing of the passions with fasting, vigils, and other mortifications. The thought of the damned falling into hell extinguished the ardor of concupiscence in him.

In 355, a revelation told Anthony that his end was near. He then undertook a visitation of the monasteries that he had founded. He exhorted his monks to continue courageously their life of piety and mortification, to flee the Arians and to keep the Faith of their fathers. Soon he stretched out and remained lying down, his face joyful as though he had seen friends coming to meet him. He died on January 17, 356. His life, recounted by his disciple and friend, St. Athanasius, has a special charm and is like a taste of heaven.

St. Anthony, help me to fight the good fight against the

flesh, the devil, and the world insofar as it is the source of temptations, and pray that I may gain interior peace, the fruit of the presence of God in my soul, and the pledge of eternal happiness.

Attributes and patronage

St. Anthony is depicted in the form of an old, bearded man, clothed in a coarse woolen robe, wielding the Egyptian cross (a T-shaped staff), with a beggar's bell and a pig at his feet. This animal symbolizes the diabolical temptations that St. Anthony successfully overcame. Sometimes he also carries a rosary or the book of the Rule of the Antonites.

He is invoked is cases of contagious illnesses and all maladies of the skin, especially shingles.

Prayer

May the intercession of the Blessed Abbot Anthony commend us, we beseech Thee, O Lord, so that what we do not deserve by any merits of ours we may obtain by his patronage. (Collect)

Thoughts

- "No one could pride himself on entering into the kingdom of heaven without having passed through temptation."

   —Maxim of St. Anthony

- "The best weapons with which to conquer the enemy are gladness and spiritual joy of the soul, which always has the presence of God in mind, because this light dispels the darkness."

   —St. Anthony, *PB*, vol. I, p. 427

Resolutions

1. Perform some work that involves giving up self-will.

2. Resort to prayer immediately in a moment of temptation.

3. During your examination of conscience, find out exactly how much time you have devoted to God and how much you have wasted on trivialities.

St. Margaret of Hungary

January 18

God speaks to us

Behind her the virgins of her train are brought to the King. They are borne in to Thee with gladness.

—Alleluia: Psalm 44:15-16

Meditation

Margaret lived in the 13th century (†1270). She was the daughter of the King of Hungary, Bela IV. She was born into a predestined family. Indeed, we find her surrounded by an impressive number of saints, both among those from whom she was descended and among her relatives who would be born after her. Her ancestors included St. Stephen, St. Stanislaus, St. Emeric (Imre). St. Hedwig was her great-aunt, St. Elizabeth—her aunt. She had as sisters St. Cunegunda as well as Blessed Yolanda and Blessed Constance. Finally, St. Louis, Bishop of Toulouse, would be the grandson of her brother and Blessed Joan of Portugal, her relative. This first feature in her life makes us realize that we are heirs. If we have the Catholic faith today, we owe it, for the most part, to the generations that preceded us. And so, let us take advantage of this feast day to show God our gratitude for having been born into a privileged setting.

Along with this grace come duties for us. We must imitate St. Margaret of Hungary, who was equal to her vocation and worthy of her ancestors. We too must make it our ideal to preserve the precious treasure that we have received and to hand it on to future generations. God has given us much, and He expects much from us in return: let us not disappoint Him!

Although St. Margaret had the grace to be born in a blessed family, she had the additional grace of making her religious profession with the Dominicans at the age of 12.

Her love for God spread to her companions, especially through the care that she lavished on those who were victims of contagious diseases. She died at the age of 28.

During her short life, she displayed many virtues to a heroic degree; she showed a great spirit of sacrifice. She lived in the utmost austerity. She wept and did penance for the misfortunes of the Church.

St. Margaret, help me to acquire the spirit of sacrifice so as to make reparation for my sins and to cooperate in the salvation of souls. Help me not to reject the cross and not to rebel against trials.

Patronage

St. Margaret is invoked especially against malaria and fevers.

Prayer

Blessed Margaret, obtain for the princes of this world an understanding that by supporting religion they defend their own interests and those of the people.

—Fr. Cormier, *AS*, p. 26

Thoughts

- "It is advisable to accept calmly the sufferings that the Lord wishes to send to us."
  —Padre Pio, *PPJ*, September 27

- "Be very submissive in the hands of the Lord. Offer Him the years that you have left to live and ask Him to make use of them according to His good pleasure."
  —Padre Pio, *PPJ*, September 13

Resolutions

1. Recite one *Magnificat*, thanking God for the treasure of being born into a Catholic family. (See Appendix.)
2. Recite the First Joyful Mystery to ask God to raise up vocations of women religious.
3. Bear patiently and charitably with the faults of family members and the infirmities caused by sickness or old age.

Our Lady of Pontmain

January 19 (celebrated on the 17th)

GOD SPEAKS TO US

Thou art the glory of Jerusalem, thou art the joy of Israel, the honor of thy people.

—Alleluia: Judith 15:10

MEDITATION

Since mankind had long since lost the Christian spirit, the Blessed Virgin appeared in Pontmain, France, on January 17, 1871, to give us a lesson in pictures. Two days ago was the anniversary of this moving apparition. The first thing that is recalled about the heavenly visitor is the message inscribed in golden letters: "Pray, my children; God will answer your prayers in a little while. My Son allows them to touch His Heart." This announcement, made in the middle of the war against the Prussians, shows the power of prayer. What consolation and what immense joy this message caused in those who witnessed it! In fact, nine days later, the armistice was signed.

Concerning this visit from heaven there is another very relevant lesson that we should remember. During one of the phases of the apparition, the Blessed Virgin appeared with her face profoundly sad, and she showed the seers her Son, bloodied on the cross. She was wearing a large red crucifix with a bleeding Christ; over Him were written these words: *"Jesus Christ."* Our Lady saw that mankind was rejecting more and more the law of suffering and was seeking enjoyment exclusively. Then, so that we might cherish the memory of what her Divine Son did for us, she presented Him to us, she showed Him to us not risen, but bloody. She wanted thereby to make us understand the intensity of His love for us. And so let us for our part show Him our gratitude.

But this episode should also remind us of our own need to take up our cross, which is very light compared to hers. May we understand her message by patiently accepting our own cross! Here on earth, every human being suffers and dies. The important thing is not to run away and to look at our cross with deep faith.

While attending the Holy Sacrifice of the Mass, let us reflect that the Precious Blood of Jesus once again comes down in the chalice.

O my Jesus, may Your Blood purify my soul and communicate to me a Christian spirit that will enable me to see my trials as an instrument of my salvation. May I imitate You so that at the moment when I return my soul to God, I might merit to see You, this time no longer bloody, but glorious in the blessed eternity of heaven.

Prayer

O God, who by the wonderful protection of the Blessed Virgin Mary didst deign to strengthen us in hope in a special way, grant that, according to her counsels, we might obtain an answer to our pious request by persevering in prayer. (Collect)

Thoughts

- "Let us take refuge with the Virgin Mary so as to await from her alone the grace to live according to the will of God and of His Son Jesus Christ."

  —Fr. Calmel, *365 J*, May 20

- "We will not lack courage, because we persevere in prayer with Mary."

  —Fr. Calmel, *365 J*, May 16

Resolutions

1 Today be sure to make the sign of the cross reverently before and after each prayer.

2 Meditate for 10 minutes on the vision of Our Lady of Pontmain, who holds and presents to us her Son on the cross.

3 Do not complain, but patiently offer to God all contradictions in a spirit of making reparation for our sins.

St. Sebastian

January 20

GOD SPEAKS TO US

God is glorious in His Saints, wonderful in Majesty, a worker of wonders.

—Gradual: Exodus 15:11

MEDITATION

St. Sebastian (†288) was the head of the first troop under Diocletian. His father was from Narbonne (Gaul) and his mother—from Milan. He performed great services for the Emperor, while very zealously supporting the Christians, particularly those who were about to waver in their faith when confronted by their persecutors.

When the Emperor learned that he was Christian, he had him tied to a post and commanded the archers to shoot their arrows at him for target practice. They left him for dead near the place of his agony. When night fell, a Christian widow who had come to bury him discovered that he was still alive. She took him home and cared for him. Very quickly his wounds healed. The Christians came to see him, begging him to go to a safe location, but far from hiding, he dared to station himself where the Emperor was about to pass by and reproached him for his cruelty to the Christians. The unexpected meeting with Sebastian terrified Diocletian, who thought that he was dead. The miraculous survivor said to him: "Mighty Emperor, they are lying to you; they are deceiving you when they tell you that we are the enemies of your empire. We are the ones supporting it by the prayers that we offer to God to preserve you." Then he added: "I live today because my Savior Jesus Christ kept me alive in order to prove by this miracle the truth of His religion. Therefore stop persecuting the saints, and if you want to live in peace, and assure your empire of long, happy days, shed no more innocent blood!"

Having recovered from his emotions, Diocletian commanded his guards to beat Sebastian to death. A holy woman had his body transported to the catacombs which now bear his name, and Pope St. Damasus, during the following century, had the magnificent Church of St. Sebastian built over his tomb.

St. Sebastian, intercede for me, that I may imitate you by strengthening the weak, by professing my faith unostentatiously but fearlessly. Pray to Jesus for me that I may experience joy in the happy awareness of being Christian and acting like one.

Attributes, invocation, and patronage

St. Sebastian is depicted with his body pierced with arrows. He is invoked especially against contagious diseases. He is the patron saint of archers and morticians.

Prayer

Have regard for our weakness, almighty God; and, since the burden of our own deeds weighs us down, let the glorious intercession of Thy Blessed Martyrs, Fabian and Sebastian, protect us. (Collect)

Thoughts

- "The true soldier of Jesus Christ , with the buckler of a living faith and the fire of charity, easily resists the cowardly attacks of pleasure, the harsh blows of torments, and the dreadful horror of death."

  —St. Sebastian, *PB*, vol. 1, p. 491

- "Sebastian, pierced with arrows, still professed his faith and preached it to his executioner: behold a good soldier of Christ."

  —St. Alphonsus Liguori, *SJJ*, p. 32

Resolutions

1. Recite a decade of the Rosary for the soldiers of your country whose lives are in danger.
2. Offer a sacrifice in order to obtain the conversion of a persecutor.
3. Encourage adolescents who are prey to doubts by showing them the beauty of our religion.

St. Agnes

January 21

God speaks to us

Sinners wait to destroy me, but I pay heed to Thy decrees, O Lord.

—Introit: Psalm 118:95

Meditation

The daughter of very rich and staunchly Christian parents, Agnes (†304), a Roman martyr, learned at a very early age to love Jesus Christ and to meditate on His life, especially His sorrowful passion. She was so beautiful and charming that the son of the Roman governor was smitten by her and wanted to marry her. But Agnes vehemently refused, telling him that she already had a spouse whose qualities were beyond comparison. Her answer caused the young man to despair. His father did not succeed either in convincing her, and when he learned that she was Christian, he tried to drag her into a house of ill repute, but the Good Lord miraculously protected her. Then they lit a pyre, but the flames left her uninjured. Finally, her head was cut off. A martyr for purity, Agnes was only 13 years old.

Our hearts are made to love God with a deep, unselfish love, a preferential love. The first commandment is to love God with our whole heart, with our whole strength, and with our whole mind, and the second is to love our neighbor as we love ourselves for the love of God. Now purity is precisely what enables us to love in an orderly fashion while seeking the true good for our neighbor. This presupposes the submission of the material part of our being to the spiritual part.

In order to be pure, we need to practice the virtue of chastity. The word *chastity* has the same root as the verb *chastise* and the noun *chastisement*. We strike an animal in order to train it and to make it behave. Similarly, chastity consists of chastising the old man, that is, checking and controlling the animal part of our being, so as to enable us to maintain self-control in all circumstances. Therefore a work of asceticism and penance is necessary in order to rein in the disordered love we have for forbidden pleasures. Concretely, we must pay close attention to what we may see or hear and rein in our imagination, so as to avoid lighting the fire of the disordered passions.

O St. Agnes, given the current surge of marital infidelities, unnatural unions, and divorces, obtain for me the grace to remain faithful to my commitments.

Attributes and patronage

St. Agnes is depicted as a child with the martyr's crown and palm branch, with a lamb beside her. She is the patron saint of virgins, fiancés, and Trinitarian religious.

Prayer

Blessed Agnes, you were beautiful to behold; but how much more beautiful you are through your faith. You despised the world; you now rejoice with the angels. Intercede for us.

—Dominican Liturgy

Thoughts

- "[Let us be] so taken by the beauty of the Lord Jesus' face that we are captivated by Him."

  —Fr. Calmel, *365 J*, January 18

- "I know my infirmity especially in this: that the most horrible fantasies take hold of my mind much more easily than they leave it."

  —*The Imitation of Christ*, Book III, chap. 20

Resolutions

1 Recite the Fourth Joyful Mystery, praying that all Catholics will courageously renounce indecent fashions.

2 Turn your glance away from any impure image and sort out your clothing.

3 Ask God for the grace of a religious vocation in your family.

St. Vincent

January 22

GOD SPEAKS TO US

Wine drunken with moderation is the joy of the soul and the heart.

—Ecclesiasticus 31:36

MEDITATION

St. Vincent (†304) belonged to a rich family in Saragossa (Spain). He could easily have risen to the highest-ranking offices in the Empire, but in his view there was a higher dignity, that of a Christian, and he wanted no other. He had just been ordained a deacon when the bloody persecution of Diocletian and Maximian broke out at the end of the third century. Since his bishop, St. Valerius, found it very difficult to express himself, he put Vincent in charge of preaching, which he did very fruitfully.

One day, when the bishop had just ascended the altar, assisted as usual by St. Vincent, a cry was heard: "Death to the Christians! Throw them to the lions! Burn them at the stake!" The governor Dacian had just issued the new edict of persecution, followed by an army of executioners, shouting cries of hatred and death.

Upon hearing these furious shouts, the young deacon calmly and seriously turned toward the Christians who were about to panic. With a solemn gesture, he called for silence, then fell to his knees before the venerable bishop: "Father," he said to him, "leave unfinished the sacred rites which you have scarcely started; deign to consecrate immediately the Eucharistic cup; give the wine of life to those whom death is seeking. Pour out for them this wine which will cure them of their alarm so that from this heavenly drink they may draw a joyful fearlessness in the face of tortures." Moved by these words, the bishop followed his deacon's advice. He consecrated the Precious Blood, and St. Vincent lifted it up for the faithful to see, saying: "Behold the Blood of Christ, behold the heavenly wine of souls!" And the faithful responded; "Yes, we believe!" Then they came to drink from the chalice that Vincent presented to them, so as to draw from it the calm resignation and the divine strength that makes martyrs.

Just then, St. Vincent was arrested with his bishop. After stretching him on a rack, Dacian had him torn with iron hooks, then roasted on a grill over a slow fire. Finally, the tortured man was laid on potshards. He was 22 years old.

O St. Vincent, help me to imitate you by working generously in the Lord's vineyard, encouraging the weak in their faith by my fidelity to prayer and by the example of my virtues.

Attributes and patronage

St. Vincent is depicted with a pruning knife and a cluster of grapes. He is the patron of vinedressers.

Prayer

We pray Thee, O Lord, grant us Thy clemency and health in soul and body. St. Vincent was faithful in his vocation as a deacon in the Church and remained one until his martyrdom. May he be our intercessor with Thee, so that we may remain true to our faith in these difficult times.

—Prayer, *PS*, vol. II, p. 346

Thoughts

- "Inebriated with the wine that makes us strong and chaste, Vincent triumphed over the tyrants who tried to ruin the kingdom of Jesus Christ."

    —St. Augustine

- "O Blood [of Christ] which fortifies the soul and removes its weakness!"

    —St. Catherine of Siena, *R*, p. 17

Resolutions

1 Recite the Litanies of the Precious Blood. (See Appendix.)

2 Draw strength from Holy Communion so as to have the courage to make yourself known as a practicing Catholic.

3 Make a resolution to avoid all abuse of alcohol (for example: no wine in the evening, on weekdays, in Advent, and during Lent...) and remember to thank the Good Lord after meals.

St. Raymond of Peñafort

January 23

GOD SPEAKS TO US

The mouth of the just man tells of wisdom and his tongue utters what is right. The law of his God is in his heart.
—Introit: Psalm 36:30-31

MEDITATION

Raymond of Peñafort (1175-1275) was born in Barcelona (Spain). He was very gifted, both physically and intellectually. He studied civil and canon law and completed his education by earning the title of doctor. Rather late in life he took the Dominican habit. His entrance into the Order of St. Dominic happened in an odd way. He counseled a member of his family against entering that religious community and then, realizing his error, tried to make amends by entering the Order himself. He was then around 45 years old and had great devotion to the Blessed Virgin. It was his exhortations that persuaded St. Peter Nolasco to found the Order of Our Lady of Mercy to ransom the captives. He was also an exemplary confessor.

A most spectacular event occurred when he was on the Island of Majorca at the same time as the king. Upon hearing about the monarch's dissolute life, Raymond decided to return to Barcelona, but the king forbade the captains of all the vessels to let him embark. St. Raymond was not discouraged. He walked toward the sea, placed his cloak on the water, and used his walking stick as a mast. Then he stood on his cloak, folding half of it up to serve as a sail. He made a crossing of 50 leagues in six hours on that improvised vessel. The number of witnesses present when the saint disembarked confirms the authenticity of this event.

The lives of the saints are very often punctuated by miracles. Since God is the Lord of nature, He can make exceptions to its laws without difficulty. Jesus, who enabled St. Peter to walk on water, granted the same power to St. Raymond. He did say, after all, "If you have faith as a grain of mustard seed, you shall say to this mountain, Remove from hence hither, and it shall remove; and nothing shall be impossible to you" (Mt. 17:19).

Grant to me, St. Raymond, to have a share in your faith, not so as to cross the sea on a cloak, but rather so as not to lose my footing in the vicissitudes of the present life, so that I may merit to arrive safe and sound at the port of eternal salvation. Amen.

Prayer

Stir up in our hearts, O Raymond, the sincere compunction that is the prerequisite for forgiveness in the sacrament of penance.

—Dom Guéranger, *AL, TN,* vol. II, p. 485

Or

You had such tender-hearted compassion for the captives; console all who languish in chains or in exile; prepare their deliverance.

—Dom Guéranger, *AL, TN,* vol. II, p. 485

Thoughts

- "It takes more time to ask for contrition than to examine your conscience.... It is indeed necessary to ask for repentance."

    —The Curé of Ars, St. John Vianney, *PPJ2*, December 10

- "Some roads seem to men to be straight, and yet they lead far away from God forever."

    —St. Benedict, *PPJ*, April 9

Resolutions

1 Recite a decade of the Rosary praying for souls that are captives to error and vice, for those who have been arrested, deported, or exiled.

2 Frequently recite the Act of Hope, especially in times of doubt or discouragement. (See Appendix.)

3 After the example of St. Raymond, profit from your mistakes so as to make progress in virtue.

St. Timothy

January 24

God speaks to us

My faithfulness and My kindness shall be with him, and through My name shall his horn be exalted.
—Offertory: Psalm 88:25

Meditation

Timothy was born in Lycaonia, in southern Asia Minor (Turkey) to a pagan father and a Jewish mother. He converted during a mission given by St. Paul in Lystra and placed himself under his direction. The Apostle to the Gentiles took him under his wing with much attention and tact, advising him, for example, to take a little wine because of his weak stomach (I Tim. 5:23). Through his mortification, Timothy wished to subject his flesh to his spirit completely.

He became the head of the Church of Ephesus, and then, since St. John's mission was to administer the various churches in Asia, he governed it with him and under his authority. The Beloved Disciple presents him as follows in the Book of the Apocalypse when he has Jesus say: "I know thy works and thy labour and thy patience and how thou canst not bear them that are evil. And thou hast tried them who say they are apostles and are not: and hast found them liars. And thou hast patience and hast endured for my name and hast not fainted" (Apoc. 2:2-3). St. John then explains that his disciple has lost his initial charity, not because he has fallen into lukewarmness, but because has not preserved the freshness of his first *Yes* to Christ.

Timothy remembered the lesson from his master; his heroic death testified to this. After St. John's departure for Rome and exile on the Island of Patmos, he governed the Church of Ephesus alone. That did not last for long, however, because he was led risk his life fighting against the false gods.

He could not bear the thought that people were offering to the devil the worship that is due to the one true God alone. One day, the inhabitants were celebrating the pagan feast day in honor of the great Diana of Ephesus, during which they marched wearing masks and armed with clubs while carrying small idols. Very soon they started to strike the passersby, wounding some and killing others. When Timothy tried to stop them, they pounced on him, pelting him with stones. Half dead, he was taken in by his disciples, who transported him to a nearby mountain, where he expired on January 24, 97 A.D.

Prayer

[St. Timothy,] to lighten the burden of your body, you subjected your senses to a rigorous penance which Paul exhorted you to ease: help us to subject the flesh to the spirit.
—Dom Guéranger, *AL, TN*, vol. II, p. 500

Or

You who went up to heaven with the martyr's halo, stretch out your palm branch to us, so that, although we are insignificant soldiers, we might be lifted up to the dwelling place where Emmanuel welcomes and crowns His elect for eternity.
—Dom Guéranger, *AL, TN*, vol. II, p. 500

Thoughts

- "Neglect not the grace that is in thee, which was given thee."

—I Timothy 4:14

- "Fight the good fight of faith. Lay hold on eternal life, whereunto thou art called."

—I Timothy 6:12

RESOLUTIONS

1. Recite five Hail Mary's as a prayer to avoid falling into routine and lukewarmness, and for the perseverance of consecrated men and women religious and of priests in their sublime vocation.
2. Entrust your soul to a spiritual guide, at least when making major decisions in your life.
3. Show children and young people the harm caused by celebrations like Halloween, by satanic music, and by novels like the Harry Potter series.

The Conversion of St. Paul

January 25

GOD SPEAKS TO US

I live, now not I: but Christ liveth in me.

—Galatians 2:20

MEDITATION

The Magi adoring the Infant Jesus symbolized the access to salvation given by Jesus to the whole human race, but who would be the laborer chosen to evangelize the pagan world? The man in question did not know Our Lord during His mortal life: a Jew who was even a persecutor of the Christians, to the point where he was present at the martyrdom of Stephen. He was born in Tarsus in Cilicia (Turkey). He received all his Christian instruction by direct revelation from Our Lord. He would even have the privilege of being caught up to the third heaven, as he relates (II Cor. 12:2). We are talking about a man named Saul, who would become St. Paul.

He ran into Jesus Christ on the road to Damascus while traveling there to persecute the Christians. Thrown to the ground from his horse by an invisible force, "he heard a voice saying to him: 'Saul, Saul, why persecutest thou Me?' He said: 'Who art thou, Lord?' And the Lord said: 'I am Jesus whom thou persecutest. It is hard for thee to kick against the goad.' And he, trembling and astonished, said: 'Lord, what wilt Thou have me to do?' And the Lord said to him: 'Arise and go into the city; and there it shall be told thee what thou must do'" (Acts 9:4-7). The experience left him blind. After three days, Ananias, a Christian from Damascus, healed him, instructed him, and baptized him. His conversion was sudden, complete, definitive, and magnificent: he is God's "vessel of election." Jesus, who saw what Paul was guilty of, saw at the same time what he was capable of.

Seemingly overnight, Paul became the great Apostle, the apostle par excellence. "Immediately he preached Jesus in the synagogues, that He is the Son of God" (Acts 9:20). Ten years before his death (†67), he had already been scourged five times by the Jews. Despite his status as a Roman citizen, he had been beaten with rods three times. In Lystra, he had been stoned and left for dead. In his voyages, he had been shipwrecked three times (II Cor. 11:25); clinging to debris from the ship, he remained for a full day and a night lost in the middle of the sea. Seven times he was thrown into prison. Faithful to God in adversity, he demonstrated by his life the intensity of God's love for generous, ardent, determined souls.

O great St. Paul, impart to us from the highest heaven some of your ardor, generosity, and magnanimity, so that we might merit one day to share your happiness in heaven.

Attributes, Invocation, and Patronage

The attributes of St. Paul are the sword of his martyrdom and the book of his Epistles. He is depicted with a noble face, a high forehead and a long beard. He is invoked against lust, hail, and snakebite. He is the patron saint of rope makers.

Prayer

O God, Thou hast taught the whole world by the preaching of Blessed Paul the Apostle; grant, we beseech Thee, that we, who today celebrate his conversion, may through his example draw nearer to Thee. (Collect)

Thoughts

- "I can do all things in Him Who strengtheneth me."
  —Philippians 4:13

- "With St. Paul I would like to say: 'I lost everything for His love, and what my soul desires is to grasp Him better each day.'"
  —Elizabeth of the Trinity, *PPJ*, January 25

THE CONVERSION OF ST. PAUL

RESOLUTIONS

1 Pray for the conversion of a relative or a friend.
2 Thank God for the grace of your baptism.
3 Strengthen your faith in Christ's divinity by studying His miracles and the prophecies about Him.

St. Polycarp

January 26

GOD SPEAKS TO US

Wonder not brethren, if the world hate you.
—First Epistle of St. John 3:13

MEDITATION

Polycarp (†169), a disciple of St. John the Evangelist, became Bishop of Smyrna (Turkey). His episcopate was tranquil enough during the reign of Trajan. He sent several of his disciples to Gaul to preach the Gospel there. He was arrested in the mid-second century. We have the account of his suffering and death thanks to the *Acts of the Martyrs*, written by eyewitnesses shortly after his death.

"When Polycarp entered the stadium, a voice from heaven was heard: 'Courage, Polycarp, and be a man.' No one saw who was speaking, but those of our group who were there heard the voice. Finally, they made him enter, and there was a great uproar when the public learned that Polycarp had been arrested. The proconsul had him brought before him and asked him if he was Polycarp. He answered yes, and the proconsul tried to make him deny his faith, saying, 'Respect your advanced age. Swear by Caesar's fortune, and change your mind.' But Polycarp eyed severely the whole crowd of impious pagans in the stadium. The proconsul insisted and said, 'Swear, and I will let you go; curse Christ.' Polycarp replied, 'I have served Him for 86 years, and He has done me no wrong; how could I blaspheme my King who saved me?' And since the proconsul insisted again and said, 'Swear by Caesar's fortune,' Polycarp replied: 'If you imagine that I will swear by Caesar's fortune, as you say, and if you pretend not to know who I am, then listen, and I will tell you clearly: I am a Christian. And if you want to learn from me the doctrine of Christianity, give me a day, and listen to me.' ... The proconsul said: 'I have animals, and I will deliver you up to them unless you change your mind.' Polycarp said: 'Call them; it is impossible for us to change our mind to go from better to worse, but it is good to change in order to go from wrong to justice.' The proconsul answered him: 'Since you scorn the beasts, I will have you burned on a pyre, unless you change your mind.' Polycarp told him: 'You threaten me with a fire that burns for a moment and shortly afterward goes out, because you do not know the fire of the judgment to come and of the eternal punishment stored up for the impious. But why delay? Go on, do what you want.'" Thus the saintly old man was burned alive, as it had been announced to him by a revelation from heaven.

Invocation

St. Polycarp is invoked against earaches because of the vision of his pillow surrounded by flames.

Prayer

O God, Thou dost gladden us by the annual feast of Blessed Polycarp, Thy Martyr and Bishop; mercifully grant that we, who venerate his heavenly birthday, may also rejoice in his protection. (Collect)

Thoughts

- "Since endless groans in Gehenna follow present joys, my dearest brethren, flee vain hilarity here, if you are afraid to weep there."
  —St. Gregory the Great, *PPJ*, January 18

- "Love heavenly goods, despise those of the earth; seek passing things not in order to enjoy pleasure but for your necessary use; this is where the Spirit leads."
  —St. Gregory the Great, *PPJ*, April 9

Resolutions

1 Recite the Fourth Glorious Mystery, asking for the grace to remain faithful to God even to the point of martyrdom, if that is your destiny.

2 Meditate for 10 minutes on the everlasting fire of hell.

3 Raise the level of the conversation in the dining hall at your workplace or the university.

St. John Chrysostom

January 27

God speaks to us

Preach the word: be instant in season, out of season: reprove, entreat, rebuke in all patience and doctrine.
—Second Epistle of St. Paul to Timothy 4:2

Meditation

John Chrysostom was born in Antioch (Turkey), around the year 344, to a well-off family of noblemen. His mother, who had been widowed at the age of 20, refused to remarry, in order to devote herself completely to his education. He returned the favor to her by his docility and filial love. Soon he took courses on rhetoric and philosophy, was an advocate for a time, then dedicated himself to the ascetical life. He received baptism at around the age of 25 from the hands of his bishop. A little later he withdrew to a monastery and lived for several years as a hermit, then, returning to Antioch, he received holy orders gradually, leading to the priesthood in 386, and finally consecration as Bishop of Constantinople (397).

As soon as he was admitted to the priesthood, he began his career as a preacher, which was so effective that he would earn the name *Chrysostom*, which means "golden mouth." In forthright language, with a wealth of practical examples, he preached morality more than dogma, defending his sheep against the ravaging wolves. Very quickly, he won the friendship of his faithful. "He looked after them, he warned them, he watched over them, and above all he loved them. Not in vague, official language, but in real life he was the father, brother, support, and friend of his people."[19]

Although he made many friends for himself, he also had many enemies. Indeed, faced with the corruption of morals, he did not hesitate to rebuke the great ones of this world for their licentious way of life. He pointed out the wicked deeds

---

[19] Ernest Hello, *Physionomies de saints* (Quebec: Variétés, 1945), 37.

of men and women in high society; he denounced the attitude of the prelates at court who were jealous of his reputation.

He dared to attack in particular the Empress Eudoxia, because she had seized the money of a widow and the field of another woman. The Empress, furious, sought to take revenge; she asked several bishops to meet in council to condemn John, but he refused to attend it.

John was compelled to go into exile, to the great regret of his people, but several prodigious miracles obliged Eudoxia to summon him back to her city. There he continued to denounce splendidly the vices of his contemporaries, so that once again he was sentenced to exile in an altogether illegal way.

Worn out by the mistreatment that he had endured along his journey to the foothills of the Caucasus, he died on September 14, 407, on the road during his deportation.

Prayer

We beseech Thee, O Lord, let Thy heavenly grace enrich Thy Church, which Thou wast pleased to adorn with the glorious virtues and teachings of Blessed John Chrysostom, Thy Confessor and Bishop. (Collect)

Thoughts

- "The characteristic feature of just men is to correct the faults of the people and to arouse in them a love for wisdom."
  —St. John Chrysostom, Commentary on Ps. 140:10

- "Let us apply ourselves to the work of our sanctification, since it is good and its object is life without end."
  —St. John Chrysostom, Commentary on Ps. 90:16

Resolutions

1 Recite a prayer of your choosing for your bishop.

2 At an opportune time, offer fraternal correction to denounce your neighbor's disorders in faith or morals.

3 Be an example for those around you at home and in school, at the university, in your workplace, and in your business.

St. Peter Nolasco

January 28

GOD SPEAKS TO US

The Son of man is not come to be ministered unto, but to minister and to give His life as a redemption for many.
—St. Matthew 20:28

MEDITATION

Born near Carcassonne, Peter Nolasco (1189-1256) lost his parents during his adolescence. In order to escape the influence of the Albigensians, which was rampant in Southern France, he went to Spain. Considering that God went so far as to become a little child in the person of Jesus Christ in order to redeem us, and agreed to die for us on a cross amid terrible sufferings, he desired to imitate Him by helping in turn his brothers in the Faith. And so he sought out those in the Church who are prey to the greatest suffering. He learned then that some Christians were abducted at sea by the Saracen pirates. He saw their bodies, victims of oppression; he saw their minds in anguish, their hearts prone to despair, and their faith endangered. Bossuet, looking at the misery of those oppressed souls, exclaimed, "My brethren, this lugubrious sight of a Christian captive in the prisons of the Mohammedans casts me into a profound meditation on the great and dreadful advances of this monstrous religion. O God! How quick the human race is to believe Satan's impostures! Alas, that the spirit of seduction and error should have influence on our reason!"[20]

In order to ransom the prisoners, St. Peter Nolasco began by selling his property. But divesting himself of his fortune has not enough for him. He wanted to do more. He wanted to imitate Our Lord by offering his own life for the deliverance of the captives. And the Blessed Virgin let him know that her Divine Son approved his sacrifice and that she wanted him to institute a religious order for this

---

[20] Bossuet, *Oeuvres oratoires*, 4:500-501.

purpose. And so the Order of Our Lady of Mercy was born, with the help of St. Raymond of Peñafort and of James I, King of Aragon.

What Bossuet said in his tribute to our hero is still as relevant as ever: "I regard the Moslem power as an indomitable ocean, always ready to inundate the Church, since its fury is stopped only by a few half-open dikes."[21] And so today more than ever we need generous souls who offer their lives for a return to the Faith of our formerly Catholic countries.

Prayer

O God, after the example of Thy charity, Thou didst divinely inspire St. Peter to enrich Thy Church with a new offspring for the redemption of the faithful; grant, by his intercession, that we may be set free from the bondage of sin, and may enjoy perpetual liberty in our heavenly home. Through our Lord.... (Collect)

Thoughts

- "If God hath so loved us, we also ought to love one another."

  —I John 4:11

- "Blessed are the merciful, for they shall obtain mercy."

  —Matthew 5:7

Resolutions

1. Recite the First Sorrowful Mystery, begging for the conversion of a Muslim.
2. Recite a *Magnificat* to thank Jesus for giving His life for us. (See Appendix.)
3. Examine your conscience to see whether you are a slave to sin, to fashion, or to anything else, and make a resolution as a result.

---

[21] *Ibid.*, p. 502.

St. Francis de Sales

January 29

GOD SPEAKS TO US

Jesus said: Learn of Me, because I am meek and humble of heart.

—St. Matthew 11:29

MEDITATION

Francis (1567-1622) was born in De Sales Castle in Savoy, of noble, virtuous parents. After studying philosophy and theology, he became a doctor of law. When ordained to the priesthood, he ministered throughout the region of Thonon-les-Bains before becoming Bishop of Geneva. He founded the Visitation Order with St. Jeanne de Chantal.

Having a lively (not to mention ardent) temperament, he stubbornly fought for at least 20 years against his inclination to anger, and attained such self-control that today he is described as "the gentle Francis de Sales." Struck by his virtue, St. Vincent de Paul testified as follows during his canonization process: "*Monseigneur* de Sales had conformed himself to Jesus so well that I wondered how a mere creature could arrive at such a degree of perfection, given human frailty. In thinking about him, I said to myself: what must God's goodness be! How good Thou art, my God, since there is so much gentleness in Thy creature, *Monseigneur* de Sales!" Without that virtue, he would never have affected souls so profoundly.

Although St. Francis de Sales converted 72,000 Protestants, he owed it above all to his holiness. This enabled him to touch the heart of God and the hearts of heretics. He combined a whole pedagogy with his prayer. Indeed, generally conversion is not the simple product of an interior illumination received directly from God. Our Lord employs human channels in order to change hearts.

In order to enlighten a soul imprisoned by error, it is absolutely necessary to know the other person's convictions, his behavior, and the truth that is to be transmitted.

Francis de Sales therefore studied Protestantism thoroughly and thus could dismantle the false principles that it contains. Employing great gentleness and tact in order to touch hearts, he exercised considerable influence on his contemporaries and remains even today a model for those who seek to convert souls imprisoned by error and vice.

Attributes and patronage

St. Francis de Sales is depicted bald and bearded, without a miter. His main attribute is a heart in flames. He is the patron saint of writers and of Catholic journalists.

Prayer

O God, by Whose will Blessed Francis, Thy Confessor and Bishop, became all things to all men for the salvation of souls, be pleased to grant, that, being filled with the sweetness of Thy love, we may be guided by his counsels and helped by his merits, and may attain to everlasting joys. (Collect)

Thoughts

- "Not only our words to our neighbor must be gentle, but also the whole interior of our soul."
 —St. Francis de Sales, *PPJ*, April 24

- "When it is necessary to contradict someone and to contrast his opinion to that of another person, we must employ great gentleness and skill, without trying to force the other person's mind."
 —St. Francis de Sales, *PPJ*, May 28

Resolutions

1 Recite a decade of the Rosary for the conversion of a Protestant.

2 Show gentleness, especially toward the unpleasant persons around us.

3 Know the main errors of Protestantism (concerning the papacy, the Mass, the Blessed Virgin, the Sacraments, Tradition…) so as to defend Catholic truth.

St. Martina

January 30

GOD SPEAKS TO US

Come, O spouse of Christ, receive the everlasting crown which the Lord has prepared for you, for Whose love you shed your blood.

—Tract

MEDITATION

St. Martina (†226) was born in Rome of illustrious parents. Her father was consul three times. Her parents had died during her youth. She inherited their wealth, but very quickly distributed it to the poor. During the reign of the Emperor Alexander, she was denounced as a Christian and had to endure a series of increasingly horrible torments: her body was torn with iron hooks, then beaten with rods, plunged into boiling oil, and thrown as food to a lion. Far from attacking her, the beast lay down peacefully at her feet.

When summoned to sacrifice to the false gods, St. Martina replied: "I have my Lord Jesus Christ who strengthens me, and I will not sacrifice at all to your demons." Upon entering the temple of Apollo, she made the sign of the cross and addressed a prayer to Our Lord. She had scarcely finished when an earthquake shook the whole city. Part of the temple fell, causing the death of the pagan priests and many followers. The idol's statue was broken into pieces. Finally, the exasperated Emperor had her beheaded. In this way Martina, triumphing over the world and hell, departed gloriously to meet her dear Spouse in heaven, our Lord Jesus Christ.

Her body was exposed for a time on the public place, but was miraculously preserved there by two eagles that prevented anyone from tampering with it. Some of her executioners were so impressed by her constancy in the midst of the most cruel treatment that they converted and merited the palm of martyrdom.

Moved by the heroic strength of the Roman saint, let us conclude our meditation by addressing this prayer to her: "Strengthen us, O Martina, so that we may never retreat [from the attacks we have to endure from the enemies of our souls], and may our trust in God always be accompanied by mistrust of ourselves."[22]

Attributes and patronage

St. Martina is depicted with the instruments of her torment, the sword and the hook. She is one of the patron saints of Rome.

Prayer

O [St. Martina], magnanimous virgin! Christian Rome commends into your hands the care of defending her. If you protect her walls, she will rest in safety. Listen to her prayers, and drive far from the holy city the enemies who might try to besiege it. She not only has to fear the battalions that thunder against her and tear down her ramparts; shadowy attacks are also made incessantly against her liberty.

—Dom Guéranger, *AL, TN*, vol. II, pp. 594-595

Thoughts

- "The way in which love proves itself is through suffering."

    —Pauline Jaricot, *PPJ*, September 6

- "Do not fear adversities! They lead the soul to the foot of the cross, and the cross brings us to the gates of heaven."

    —Padre Pio, *PPJ*, March 17

Resolutions

1 Make reparation for your thoughts of disordered self-love by invoking the Sacred Heart.

2 Imitate the courage of St. Martina in dealing with your detractors.

3 Make a donation to a good work.

---

[22] Dom Guéranger, *AL, TN*, vol. II, p. 595.

St. John Bosco

January 31

God speaks to us

God gave him wisdom and understanding exceeding much, and largeness of heart as the sand that is on the seashore.
—Introt: Third Book of Kings 4:29

Meditation

John Bosco (1815-1888) was born in a village in the Piedmont region in Italy. His mother, a humble woman who had remained a widow, was illiterate but highly virtuous, and she made of every opportunity to raise her three children. "On every occasion she reminded them of the presence of a great witness of our actions, our thoughts: a witness who tomorrow will be the judge: 'God sees you, my little ones,' she repeated. 'God sees you. I may be absent, but He is always there.'"[23] John Bosco, while still very young, amused the boys on feast days by his prestidigitation and then brought them to church for the divine offices and to learn the catechism. Endowed with an extraordinary memory, he used to repeat the sermons that he had heard in church.

He went to Don Cafasso for spiritual direction and decided very early to give his life to God, dedicating it to the service of children and adolescents. "I will love them and will earn their love," he used to say. In order to do that, he made precise resolutions at the moment when he started his mission: "Firm resolutions to desire what is good and to prevent evil, but gentleness and prudence in order to achieve this twofold purpose. Let us seek to make ourselves loved before making ourselves feared. Wait until we are in control of ourselves before punishing. Set aside anything that could suggest that you are acting under the influence of passion. No agitation in our hearts, no disdain in our looks, no insults on our lips. Let us have compassion for now, and hope for the future. Then we will be true fathers and we

---

[23] Augustin Auffray, *St. John Bosco* (Bollington-Macclesfield: Savio, 1964), 21.

will bring about a genuine amendment."

After he was ordained a priest in Turin in 1841, he founded the Institute of the Salesians to relieve the poverty of neglected youngsters by providing them with healthy amusements, instructing them, forming workshops, and leading them in prayer. He also wisely published books and brochures so as to hand on sound doctrine. He encountered obstacles of all sorts in gaining acceptance by the civil and religious authorities, but finally he won his case. He was also the founder of the Institute of the Daughters of Mary Auxiliatrix.

Patronage

St. John Bosco is the patron saint of apprentices and of Catholic editors.

Prayer

O God, Thou didst raise up St. John, Thy Confessor, to be a father and teacher of youth, and didst will that through him, with the help of the Virgin Mary, new families should flourish in Thy Church; grant, we beseech Thee, that, inflamed by the same fire of love, we may labor to seek souls and serve Thee alone. (Collect)

Thoughts

- "O eternity! The only thing worthy of my thoughts and care, why was I able to forget you until now?"
  —St. John Bosco, *MDB*, p. 37
- "If you want your life to be full of joy and peace, you must seek to remain in God's grace."
  —St. John Bosco, *PDB*, p. 24

Resolutions

1 Live more in the presence of God by praying, especially before starting work and when you travel.

2 Take the time to listen to young people and give them appropriate advice at the opportune moment.

3 Correct your neighbors (at home or at work) only when you are completely in control of yourself in the sight of God.

St. Ignatius of Antioch

February 1

GOD SPEAKS TO US

Think and do whatever is holy, following the example that I gave you.

—Based on Philippians 4:8-9

MEDITATION

In order to strengthen our faith, it is good for us to re-immerse ourselves in its purest source by going back to the persecutions of the Apostles and their spiritual sons. Ignatius (d. 107) was born in Antioch (Turkey), which was then the most important city in the Middle East. At the death of St. Evodius, to whom St. Peter had entrusted the city upon his departure, the faithful and their pastors chose Ignatius to succeed him as their bishop. He had to fight against the Docetists, a sect that refused to recognize the humanity of Christ. Christ—according to these heretics—had only the appearance of a human body. Consequently, they refused to be fed by the Holy Eucharist. Ignatius preached to them the two natures of Christ, human and divine, and His Real Presence in the Eucharist. But soon, under the Emperor Trajan (98-117), following the era of tranquility during the reign of Nerva (96-98), a new persecution against the Christians began. In January 107, Ignatius was arrested and condemned to be thrown to wild animals. His martyrdom was to take place in Rome, and so he had to endure a long and painful journey lasting 11 months. Ignatius took advantage of it to edify the Christian communities along the way.

While he was traveling, he feared that some influential men might intervene to obtain his release. So he hastened to write to the Church of Rome this moving letter: "It has been a good start; let nothing prevent me from obtaining the inheritance reserved for me. Your charity is what I fear; you, for your part, have nothing to lose. As for me, I lose God if you succeed in saving me. I will never again find such an opportunity to reunite with Him." Then he added:

I write to the Churches: I send word to you all that I want to die for God, if you do not prevent me. I implore you not to show untimely affection. Let me be the food of beasts, by which it will be granted to me to enjoy God. I am God's wheat; I must be ground by the teeth of beasts, in order to be found the pure bread of Christ. Entice them instead, that they may be my tomb, that they may leave nothing of my body, and that my funeral may not burden anyone.[24]

When he arrived in Rome, Trajan's triumph over the Dacians was being celebrated. Thousands of victims were needed for the amusement of the people, because the festivities lasted 123 days. On December 20, 107, Ignatius was delivered to the wild beasts and became, according to his wishes, "God's wheat."

Prayer

Look down upon our weakness, almighty God; and since the weight of our own deeds bears us down, may the glorious intercession of Blessed Ignatius, Thy Bishop and Martyr, protect us. (Collect)

Thoughts

- "Let us perform all our actions with the thought that God dwells in us: we will thus be His temples, and He will be our God."
    —St. Ignatius, Epistle to the Ephesians, Ch. 15

- "Unless the grain of wheat falling into the ground die, itself remaineth alone. But if it die, it bringeth forth much fruit."
    —John 12: 24b-25a

---

[24] St. Ignatius of Antioch, Epistle to the Romans, Ch. 4.

RESOLUTIONS

1. Meditate for 10 minutes on the words of The Apostles Creed, then recite it with all your heart.
2. Patiently accept the contradictions we endure because of our faith.
3. Make a communion of reparation for the lack of reverence of our contemporaries towards the Holy Eucharist.

The Presentation of Jesus at the Temple

February 2

GOD SPEAKS TO US

And after the days of her purification, according to the law of Moses, were accomplished, they carried Him to Jerusalem, to present Him to the Lord:

—Luke 2:22

MEDITATION

While slaves of the Egyptians, the Hebrews begged for a liberator, and God raised up Moses to lead them to the promised land. But it took the ten plagues of Egypt, the last of which was the death of the firstborn of the Egyptians, to win the consent of the pharaoh to let them go. While the firstborn of the Hebrews were protected by the blood of the lamb smeared on the lintel of the doors of their houses, the firstborn of the Egyptians were exterminated by the angel of God. Since then, in thanksgiving for this special protection of God, the Hebrews made the offering of their eldest sons, according to what is written in the Book of Numbers: "The Lord spoke to Moses, saying: The day on which I slew every firstborn in the land of Egypt, I consecrated to Myself all the firstborn of Israel" (based on Exodus 13:1-2 and 15).

It is therefore with dispositions of obedience and thanksgiving that Our Lady submitted to this law today. Of course, she did not wait for that day to offer her Son to God interiorly. She already offered Him from the day of the conception of Jesus in her womb. But today she expressed in a visible way the interior state of her soul.

In an act of unprecedented magnanimity, she offered Our Lord to God His Father. And she offered Him not only as an individual, as a simple Israelite, but as Head of the future mystical body which is the Church. As a result, we are already present at this offering. It is not an exaggeration to think that if offering her divine Son for the salvation of the world, Our Lady is already thinking of all the souls who will benefit from the fruits of His Passion.

Through this offering, made with such beautiful dispositions, she perfectly met God's expectation. Today, as on the day of the Annunciation, she renewed her *Fiat*: "Be it done to me according to Thy word" (Lk. 1:38). At this offering was when the old man Simeon announced that her Son would be "a sign of contradiction" (Lk. 2:34) and, as for Our Lady, a "two-edged sword of sorrow shall pierce her soul" (Lk. 2:35).

Prayers

Purify my soul, O Lord, so that it can be totally flooded by Your light and Your love. Through our Lord.

—Fr. Gabriel of St. Mary Magdalen, *ID*, II, p. 6

Or

O obedient Virgin! May your prompt obedience serve as forgiveness for our rebellion, may it be easy for us in all things to follow your holy example.

—St. Joan of France, *R*, p. 11

Thoughts

- "Let us therefore unite ourselves with the Blessed Virgin offering her Son, and let us offer with her this Holy Child, this chosen one of God, in whom God is well pleased. Let us offer Him for our sins; let us offer Him as the divine Lamb who bears the sins of the world; as the true Son of God, who alone is pleasing in his eyes."

    —Fr. Chevrier, *R*, p. 11

- "Oh, how happy are the souls who are who belong entirely to God and who can truly say: Jesus is all my good and I am all his."

    —St. Jane Frances de Chantal, *R*, p. 11

The Presentation of Jesus at the Temple

Resolutions

1. Recite the Fourth Joyful Mystery of the Rosary.
2. Read in your missal the prayers for the Blessing of Candles and meditate a few minutes on them. Light the candles during your evening prayers.
3. Respond to the love of Jesus and Mary by prompt and joyful obedience.

St. Blaise

February 3

God speaks to us

And all that will live godly in Christ Jesus shall suffer persecution.

—II Timothy 3:12

Meditation

As Lent approaches, the Church commends to us examples of numerous martyrs. These show us by their life of sacrifice how far God's love leads.

Today we celebrate St. Blaise. At first a physician, then Bishop of Sebaste in Armenia (Turkey), he ended up withdrawing to a mountain to lead a solitary life there.

Blaise lived in a cave where wild animals familiarly came near him; he blessed them and healed those who were sick. He had a power over the animals similar to that of Adam before the Fall. During a persecution soldiers came looking for him. He was thrown into prison and beaten with rods because he refused to sacrifice to idols. A pious woman brought him food to eat and asked him in exchange to pray for her and to help her in her trials. The saint's reputation only spread farther, so that people brought the sick to him so that he might heal them. One day Blaise was visited by an inconsolable mother whose son was on the brink of death. A fish bone was stuck in the boy's throat and he was dying. Moved by this woman's tears, the saint prayed to Jesus to restore health to her child and the prayer was answered immediately. Blaise appeared a second time before the governor. He was beaten again with rods, then torn with iron combs on the rack. Under the blows, he blessed God who gave him the strength to overcome his torments and the courage to endure something for love of Him.

When he was thrown into a lake near Sebaste, Blaise made the sign of the cross, walked on the waters, and returned to the shore. In his fury the governor ordered the executioners to cut off his head (d. ca. 316). With Blaise, they killed two young Christians who had courageously professed faith in Christ.

O St. Blaise, in this period of apostasy, help me never to be ashamed of my faith, but let me profess it courageously without fear of being criticized or mocked by my neighbors.

Patronage and Invocation

St. Blaise is the patron saint of wool weavers, construction workers, and stonemasons. He is especially invoked against whooping cough, goiter, and sore throat. On his feast day, it is possible to receive a special blessing from a priest who invokes the saint while holding two blessed candles crossed over our throat to ward off illness. St. Blaise is also invoked to preserve animals.

Prayer

O God, who dost gladden us by the annual feast of blessed Blaise, Thy Martyr and Bishop, mercifully grant that we who celebrate his heavenly birthday, may also rejoice in his protection. (Collect)

Thoughts

- "Accept annoying events, adore Divine Providence, follow it, do not step over it."
  —St. Vincent de Paul, *PPJ*, September 23

- "The grace of perseverance is the most important of all: it crowns all the graces."
  —St. Vincent de Paul, *PPJ*, July 26

Resolutions

1. Pray three times the Collect for the Mass of St. Blaise (above) for persons suffering from throat cancer or other illnesses for which his intercession is invoked.

2. Respect animals as creatures of God.

3. Recount the life of a holy martyr to a person in your circle of friends to show him the power of grace.

St. Joan of France

February 4

God speaks to us

Be ye kind one to another; merciful, forgiving one another, even as God hath forgiven you in Christ.

—Ephesians 4:32

Meditation

The life of Joan of France (1464-1504) is placed under the sign of suffering. By birth—as the daughter of King Louis XI—she seemed destined for glory, and yet her life was a veritable Calvary.

Louis XI was an unscrupulous king. In the Spring of 1464, his wife, Charlotte of Savoy, was expecting her fifth child, but the first three had died and the fourth was a daughter, Anne of Beaujeu. The king was persuaded that Charlotte was at last going to give him a boy to succeed him, but the queen gave birth to little Joan. The king was furious. One month later, having calculated the political advantages of marrying his daughter to Louis of Orléans, then two years old, he betrothed them. Physicians detected in Joan a deviation of the spinal column that would later cause her to limp. This only intensified her father's harshness towards her. At the age of five, she was entrusted to the care of François de Beaujeu, Baron of Lignières, and his wife. Joan stayed with them until the age of 20, but when she was 12 years old—which was the legal age to contract a marriage—Louis XI announced his plan to make her marry the Duke of Orléans. She eventually submitted to her father's will, but Louis of Orléans was not so compliant. However, despite the refusal of the then fourteen-year-old duke, the marriage was decided and contracted on September 8, 1476. Married against his will, Louis of Orléans did not manage to grow fond of his wife, who suffered cruelly as a result. Nevertheless, she redoubled her efforts to love him with all her heart. After the king's death in 1483, she went to Amboise, where Anne of Beaujeu was regent for her younger brother, Charles VIII. During this time of chaos, Louis of Orléans went to war against Charles VIII and was captured at Bourges. His wife did everything she could to have him released, and eventually she succeeded. Once he had become king, Louis XII had the tribunal of the Church acknowledge the nullity of his marriage. For Joan, this was her most devastating trial. However, she bore it valiantly. Louis XII gave Joan the Duchy of Berry and she founded the Order of the Annunciades in order to spend the rest of her life in prayer, work, and self-giving. To avoid the snare of pride, Joan wore a rough hair shirt under her cloth-of-gold dress. She cared for plague victims with her own hands. Finally, at the age of 40, she died in the peace of God.

Prayer

Blessed St. Joan, more illustrious for being the bride of Jesus Christ than for the blood of kings from whom you descended, you were the sanctuary of all the virtues and always cherished by your Spouse. By your merits, grant that we may persevere in doing His will.

—Prayer, *PS*, p. 184

Thoughts

- "Do not believe men thoughtlessly when their words go against others and excuse those about whom others speak badly."

  —St. Joan of France, *LP*, 1950

- "Strive to make peace reign among all those around you who are in some dispute or enmity."

  —St. Joan of France, *LP*, 1950

Resolutions

1 Pray a decade of the Rosary and ask St. Joan of France to intercede so that France will recover its Catholic roots.

2 Pray the *Memorare* for spouses who cannot get along. (See appendix.)

3 Practice patience in adversity to triumph over evil by good with the help of St. Joan of France.

St. Agatha

February 5

God speaks to us

God is in the midst of His city, it shall not be moved: God will help it in the morning early.

—Psalm 45:6

Meditation

Born in Sicily in Catania or in Palermo in 251, St. Agatha endured martyrdom under the Emperor Decius.

Governor Quintianus fell very passionately in love with Agatha. When she was interrogated by him at his tribunal, she declared: "I am a free woman, of a noble family; all my relatives are here to attest to that." She was, in effect, free with the liberty of the children of God, emancipated from the devil, from sin, from slavery to fashion, and from what might be said about her. Because of this freedom, she said *no* to sin, refusing to submit to an unjust law. While her judge begged her to offer incense to idols, she replied: "I keep a profound worship for my holy freedom. It consists of liberation from evil, your passions, your idols, your gold, and your pleasures. You are imposing slavery on me; I do not want it. I accept only the slavery of Jesus, whose yoke is so gentle and whose burden is light."

Impiety, inspired by the devil, cannot stand those who profess the true faith, those who love Jesus Christ with all their heart, hence Quintianus' stubborn attempts to snatch from Agatha's soul her faith in Jesus Christ. The governor sought to pervert her ideas and corrupt her morals. Today the devil's strategy remains the same and still produces as many victims. For one month Agatha was imprisoned with Aphrodite, an immoral woman who tried to corrupt her, but she stood firm. Losing patience with her tenacity, Quintianus made Agatha endure various tortures. Slapped, thrown into prison, tortured on the rack, she refused to sacrifice to idols. Infuriated, Quintianus ordered the mutilation of her breasts. Indignant, she said to him: "Barbarian, so you have even desecrated your mother's memory! But I have conserved all the integrity of my soul that I consecrated to the Lord Jesus since my childhood." However, an old man appeared to her the following night and miraculously healed her, leaving no trace of her wounds. The governor, furious at seeing her healed, ordered that Agatha be rolled on broken glass and burning coals. At last, raising her eyes to heaven, she let out a great cry and gave up the ghost. Later, on various occasions, exhibiting her veil during the eruption of Mount Etna was enough to protect the neighboring cities.

Patronage and Invocation

St. Agatha is the patron saint of wet nurses. She is invoked against breast pain, against fires or misfortunes caused by fire.

Prayer

O God, let us be protected from all evil, especially from the harmful fire, the fire of passion, and eternal fire, through the intercession of St. Agatha. Through our Lord Jesus Christ.

—Prayer, *PS*, vol. I, p. 7

Thoughts

- "Although trials in themselves are cruel, the love and inner ardor of the soul soften them."
  —St. Thomas Aquinas, *PPJ*, August 11
- "He who has suffered and fought for his God will shine like a beautiful sun."
  —St. John Vianney, *PPJ2*, November 27

Resolutions

1 Pray a decade of the Rosary for those who suffer the consequences of a fire in their body or in the loss of property.

2 Dare to denounce the slavery of evil and always prefer to it the field of freedom that God has reserved for us.

3 Keep in your wardrobe only what is consistent with your dignity as a child of God.

St. Dorothy

February 6

GOD SPEAKS TO US

The Lord God hath opened my ear so that I may hear His voice; whatever He says, I do not resist: I have not gone back.
—Based on Isaias 50: 5

MEDITATION

The Church proposes for our meditation the beautiful figure of Dorothy († *ca.* 311), Virgin and Martyr. By her life and above all by her glorious death, we see how far a soul faithful to grace can go. In her is fulfilled the prediction made by God to Satan: "I will put an enmity between you and the woman, between your offspring and her offspring" (Gen. 3:15). Above all the Blessed Virgin is this woman, but so are the women who lived fully under the regime of grace, especially the virgin martyrs. These holy women are truly the honor of the Church. We are proud of them! The devil knows that he has everything to fear from a woman who is fervent, valiant, pure, and docile to grace. That is why he has been attacking women so relentlessly for two centuries by perverting them. Therefore let us recover our strength today by contemplating the heroic virtues of Dorothy.

She was born at Caesarea in Cappadocia (Turkey). Physically very beautiful, Dorothy shone with her virtues. She was chaste, temperate, quite gentle, humble, and remarkably wise. Arrested as a Christian by Governor Apricius, Dorothy was subjected to torture. First stretched on the rack, she then had her sides burnt by flaming torches. Then they brought two women who had apostatized to convince Dorothy to deny Christ, but far from being shaken by them, she converted them.

Finally, her judge sentenced her to be struck with a sword. As Dorothy was being led to the place of her torment, she made this prayer: "Receive my thanksgiving, O friend of souls, Who has deigned to call me to the delights of Your paradise." A pagan named Theophilus heard her and mockingly said, "Come, bride of Christ, send me apples or roses from the paradise of your husband"; she replied, "Certainly I will." Since her answer had been dictated to her by the Holy Ghost, Theophilus converted immediately and was martyred in turn.

O St. Dorothy, support us in our combat against the devil.

Attributes

St. Dorothy is depicted with a basket decorated with flowers, carried by angels or by the Infant Jesus.

Prayer

May blessed Dorothy, Thy Virgin and Martyr, we beseech Thee, O Lord, obtain pardon for us: for she merited Thy constant good pleasure by her life of chastity, attributed by her to Thy power. (Collect)

Thoughts

- "All that is done for love is love; sorrow and even death are only love, when we receive them for love."
  —St. Francis de Sales, *PPJ*, August 14

- "Lean on the cross of Christ, following the example of Mary. You will find great comfort in it."
  —Padre Pio, *PPJ*, May 12

Resolutions

1 Pray the prayer above and add five *Hail Mary's* to it for the virtue of purity.

2 Make sure to mortify your eyes to preserve the virtue of purity.

3 Decorate with flowers the statue of a saint in your house or your church while asking his protection an invoking him several times during the day.

St. Romuald

February 7

GOD SPEAKS TO US

And they that are Christ's, have crucified their flesh, with the vices and concupiscences.

—Galatians 5:24

MEDITATION

Romuald (906-1027) was born at Ravenna (Italy) to a noble family. During his youth, he indulged in a life of pleasure. Forced to attend a duel during which his father killed his opponent, Romuald felt partly responsible and wanted to make amends by spending 40 days in a monastery, doing extreme penances. There, a brother persuaded him to dedicate himself totally to God. After living for seven years in a Benedictine monastery where he became an exemplary religious, Romuald retired to solitude near a hermit named Marin, who proved to be a very severe man.

Romuald's heart, reborn through penance, became inflamed with a desire for martyrdom. He left for Pannonia with the intention of dying for the Faith, but health problems forced him to turn back. God had other plans for him. He destined Romuald to found a religious family: the Order of Camaldolese Hermits.

This community had the unique feature of allowing some members to lead an eremitic life alongside other brothers living in community. Like the patriarch Jacob, he saw a ladder rising from earth to heaven, by which men dressed in white went up and down. This vision foretold the marvelous fruits that would result from his order.

Romuald pursued his life of renunciation and prayer. God tested his virtue through repeated attacks by the devil, who asked Romuald, "What use are so many prayers and penances?" The saint's victories only infuriated the devil more, to the point where Romuald was beaten and trampled underfoot by infernal spirits taking the most horrible forms. Though assailed by so many trials, St. Romuald, far from appearing sad, always remained smiling and joyous.

An athlete of penance, Romuald lived, despite his spectacular austerities, to the age of 120 years, of which almost 100 were passed in the service of God. His body was found incorrupt 440 years after his death, with a sweet and venerable face.

O St. Romuald, model of penance and of the spirit of prayer, awaken in me the spirit of sacrifice as Lent approaches, and help me to detach myself from the world so as to live more in the presence of God.

Attributes

St. Romuald is depicted wearing the white habit of the Camaldolese Hermits, with a heavenly ladder on which his monks climb to heaven, or else with a finger in front of his mouth to express his profound love of silence.

Prayer

May the intercession of blessed Romuald the Abbot commend us unto Thee, we beseech Thee, O Lord: so that what we cannot acquire by any merits of ours, we may obtain by his patronage. (Collect)

Thoughts

- "It is better to say, if possible, a single psalm with heart and compunction than a hundred with a rambling mind."

  —St. Romuald, *PL* 144, 964c

- "Dearest Jesus, so dear, my honey and my sweetness, my inexpressible desire, sweetness of saints, delight of angels!"

  —St. Romuald, *PL* 144, 983ab

Resolutions

1 Pray a decade of the Rosary that the Good Lord will raise up fervent religious.

2 Carefully place yourself in the presence of God as you start to pray.

3 Deprive yourself of one food during your next meal.

St. John of Matha

February 8

God speaks to us

Be ye therefore merciful, as your Father also is merciful.
—Luke 6:36

Meditation

John of Matha (1154-1213) saw the light of day in Faucon (Alpes de Haute-Provence). From his earliest childhood, he showed signs of great piety and charity to the poor. He studied theology in Paris. At the moment of his priestly ordination, when the bishop imposed his hands on John and said to him: "Receive the Holy Spirit," a pillar of fire appeared on John's head, a sign that the Third Person of the Trinity had taken possession of his soul.

On the day of his first Mass, at the elevation of the host, his face was radiant. A white angel in human form appeared to John, carrying on his breast a red and blue cross. He offered his hands to two captives, one Christian, the other Muslim; they knelt at his feet, begging. This was the announcement of his mission as founder of the Order of Trinitarians for the redemption of captives. Pope Innocent III later had the same vision and therefore had no difficulty approving his order. Faithful to his mission, St. John of Matha made several journeys among the infidels and by his steadfast faith overcame the persecutions and obstacles that the devil set against his charity. God supported his zeal with miracles. One day, returning from Tunis with the slaves he had freed, having just set sail, he was attacked by barbarians. His boat no longer had a sail, oars, or rudder. The saint invoked the Blessed Virgin, then he extended his cloak as a sail. The ship was soon sailing on the open sea and arrived at the port of Ostia in less than two days, to the astonishment of a bewildered crowd. John then continued to travel through Italy, France, and Spain, building monasteries everywhere. In Spain he liberated a large number of Christians who had been captured by the Saracens. The

St. John of Matha

King of France, Philip Augustus, took John for his chaplain and confessor. To touch the heart of God, he joined prayer and penance to faith. He slept very little and wore a rough hair shirt and an iron chain around his waist. Worn out by fatigue, John completed his earthly pilgrimage at Rome, where he peacefully rendered his soul to God.

Invocation

St. John of Matha is invoked for all the captives of today: those persecuted for their faith, those whose faith is in danger, slaves of any passion.

Prayer

O God, Who through St. John didst from heaven deign to institute the Order of the Most Holy Trinity for ransoming captives from the power of the Saracens: help us through his merits, we beseech Thee, to freedom from bondage of body and of soul. (Collect)

Thoughts

- "The saints are holy because they walked in the footsteps of Our Lord, renounced themselves, and mortified themselves in all things."
  —St. Vincent de Paul, *PPJ*, November 1

- "Let us always bear in mind the misfortunes and sufferings of the world in order to alleviate them."
  —Padre Pio, *PPJ*, October 26

Resolutions

1 Pray a decade of the Rosary to beg for the cure of a drug addict or an alcoholic.

2 Recite three times with a great spirit of adoration the prayer *Glory Be* in honor of the Holy Trinity.

3 Take definite measures to avoid addiction to the Internet (time spent, objectionable websites) or to a mobile phone (SMS, time spent, and the company you keep).

St. Cyril of Alexandria

February 9

God speaks to us

And in nothing be ye terrified by the adversaries: to them [their persecutions are] a cause of perdition, but to you of salvation, and this from God.

—Philippians 1:28

Meditation

Cyril of Alexandria († 444) lived during a particularly troubled period in Church history. His uncle Theophilus, Bishop of Alexandria, detested a community of monks called "big brothers," who nevertheless gave the finest example of religious virtues. St. John Chrysostom welcomed these religious in his entourage, which made Theophilus furious with him. As a witness to the dispute, Cyril sided with his uncle, but Pope Innocent I took up the cause of the religious and of St. John Chrysostom. The Holy Father excommunicated Theophilus, who eventually repented before his death. Cyril succeeded his uncle in the episcopal see. Despite his uprightness, he still had reservations about the "big brothers," and to dispel his doubts he prayed wholeheartedly to the Blessed Virgin. The story goes that St. John Chrysostom appeared to him and gave him threatening looks, urging him to leave office unless he repented of his prejudices. The Blessed Virgin then interceded in favor of Cyril and obtained his pardon.

Our Lady had saved our saint. He would repay her. Indeed, the Blessed Virgin's honor was soon attacked by a heretic named Nestorius. He claimed that Our Lady was the mother of Jesus in His humanity, but not the Mother of God. At the Council of Ephesus (431), more than 200 bishops met again to decide the question, headed by St. Cyril as the Pope's legate. There Mary was proclaimed Mother of God. The error was crushed, Nestorius was deposed. Unfortunately, Nestorius would not submit and died unrepentant. Leaving Ephesus to travel back to his episcopal see, Cyril passed the rest of his life fulfilling his duties as a bishop, preserving the treasure of the faith in all its purity, re-establishing the peace that had been troubled by heresy, and defending the integrity of morals. His writings show such depth and clarity that he is called "the Seal of the Fathers." After governing the Church of Alexandria for 32 years, he rejoined Our Lord and His holy Mother in the blessed eternity of heaven.

Attributes

St. Cyril is depicted seated and giving a blessing, with the Blessed Virgin above him in the air, holding the Child on her breast, or else a book in her hand and a dove on her shoulder.

Prayer

O God, Who didst make blessed Cyril, Thy Confessor and Bishop, the invincible champion of the divine Motherhood of the most Blessed Virgin Mary: grant that by his intercession, we who believe her to be truly the Mother of God, may be saved by her motherly protection. (Collect)

Thoughts

- "The Blessed Virgin can be called both Mother of Christ and Mother of God, because she brought into the world not a man like us, but the Word of the Father who was incarnate and became man."
  —St. Cyril of Alexandria, *PG77*, 13, 21, 64

- "The *Hail Mary* is the most beautiful prayer after the *Our Father*: it is a prayer that never wearies."
  —The Curé of Ars, *PPJ2*, October 6

Resolutions

1 Pray five *Hail Mary's*, paying attention to the words "Mother of God."

2 Do not return to a quarrel.

3 Come to the defense of the Blessed Virgin when she is attacked.

St. Scholastica

February 10

God speaks to us

A faithful friend is a strong defense: and he that hath found him, hath found a treasure.

—Ecclesiasticus 6:14

Meditation

A true friendship is one that leads each of the two friends to desire the good of the other, not a search for self-satisfaction. It is a blessing that soothes our sojourn in this land of exile. What grace to have near us an open heart, always ready to listen to us, a heart ready to share our joys and our sorrows. St. Scholastica (480-543) had the benefit of this treasure. Her blood brother, Benedict, was a support for her throughout her life. "St. Gregory tells us that the sister's soul had always been, not united, but one with her brother's soul. A wonderful unity, all for the benefit of the brother who loved the sister, all for the benefit of the sister, who loved the brother."[25]

St. Scholastica was born at Nursia (Umbria, Italy). She consecrated herself to God from early childhood and became close to her brother when he settled at Monte Cassino with his monks. To profit from his lessons and example, she founded the Order of Benedictine nuns. St. Benedict saw his sister only once a year, shortly before Lent. They would meet halfway on the mountainside. On February 9, 543, Scholastica was faithful to the annual meeting. The day passed very quickly, as usual, to the point that night surprised them. St. Benedict wished to part from his sister, but she urged him to continue during the night their sweet conversation about the joys of paradise. He retorted that it was not in keeping with the Rule to spend the night outside his abbey. Scholastica then started to pray, and immediately a violent storm prevented Benedict from leaving. So,

---

[25] Father Emmanuel, *Méditations* (Dismas, 1987), 355.

the two saints stayed up all night talking about the happiness of the elect. The next day they parted, and three days later St. Benedict saw his sister's soul fly up to heaven in the form of a dove.

May we, in turn, draw true comfort from friendship, while waiting to join St. Benedict and St. Scholastica in heaven one day.

"O beloved saint Scholastica, make our hearts enter into the unity of your heart, teach us to love, to love the Divine Spouse, to love one another in Him and for Him."[26]

Invocation and Patronage

St. Scholastica is invoked against storms, to pray for rain and to cure sleepwalking. She is the patroness of the city of Le Mans.

Prayer

O God, Who, to show us the way of innocence, didst cause the soul of Thy blessed Virgin Scholastica to enter heaven in the form of a dove: grant through her merits and prayers that we may live in an innocence that will win for us eternal joys. (Collect)

Thoughts

- "In prosperity we cannot recognize the true friend."
  —Sirach 12:8

- "He who is a friend loves all the time, and it is in affliction that he reveals himself to be a brother."
  —Proverbs 17:17

Resolutions

1 Pray a decade of the Rosary for your best friend.

2 Think about your choice of friends and break off with false friends.

3 Be sure to have edifying conversations with friends and to avoid gossip.

---

[26] *Ibid.,* p. 356.

Our Lady of Lourdes

February 11

GOD SPEAKS TO US

Hail, full of grace, the Lord is with thee; blessed art thou amongst women.

—Offertory: Luke 1:28

MEDITATION

On February 11, 1858, in the land of France, which is the kingdom of Mary—*Regnum Galliae, Regnum Mariae*—in Lourdes, a fourteen-year-old child, Bernadette Soubirous, went to gather wood with some friends to supply the household of her impoverished parents. As she prepared to cross the River Gave, she saw in the crevice of a rock a beautiful lady whose gentle gaze fascinated her, immobilizing her. The Lady was clothed in a magnificent white dress with a sky-blue sash. She held in her hand a rosary and was fingering the beads. On each of her feet, which hardly seemed to rest on a wild rose bush, a beautiful rose blossomed. She appeared eighteen times between February 11 and July 16, 1858.

Since France—the eldest daughter of the Church—had progressively abandoned her religious convictions, the Blessed Virgin came there to revive the Faith. She traveled to earth to remind rationalist man of the existence of the invisible world. Indeed, if the Blessed Virgin appeared right in the middle of the 19th century, it was to remind us that there is a life after this life.

During an era when man, imbued with scientism and in quest of unbridled liberty, ceaselessly repeated: "Pleasure, pleasure, pleasure," the Blessed Virgin came down from heaven to say to him: "Penance, penance, penance." But why do penance? Our Lady implied the answer in pronouncing these words on March 25: "I am the Immaculate Conception." If she is not "an" immaculate woman, but the Immaculate, it is because she alone was not soiled by sin. As for us, we are sinners. We must, then, extinguish by penance the fire of sin that is in us. The Blessed Virgin also set for us the example of reciting the Rosary by letting the beads slip through her fingers, while Bernadette recited the Hail Mary's, and she joined her little confidante in saying the Glory Be's with her. Thus she showed us how much she cherishes those who pray to her. And she supported the authenticity of her coming by making water spring from the rock: water that has produced many astounding miracles, both physical by curing diseases, and moral by numerous conversions. 67 have been officially recognized to date, but a thousand cases remain unexplained.

So, let us pray fervently to Mary. Let us entrust our intentions to her and we ourselves will experience the effectiveness of her prayer to Jesus, her divine Son, who lives and reigns with the Father and the Holy Ghost, world without end.

Prayer

O God, Who by the Immaculate Conception of the Virgin didst prepare a worthy dwelling for Thy Son: we humbly beseech Thee, that we, who celebrate the Apparition of this same Blessed Virgin, may obtain health of soul and body. (Collect)

Thoughts

- "If you knew what I saw there! If you knew how good the Blessed Virgin is!"

    —St. Bernadette, *PPJ*, February 20

- "Give me the grace to love Jesus and Mary as they want to be loved."

    —St. Bernadette, *PPJ*, March 8

Resolutions

1 Pray with the utmost attention a decade of the Rosary, or even an entire Rosary in honor of Our Lady.

2 Make a sacrifice by depriving yourself of dessert at a meal.

3 Decorate a statue or an image of Our Lady.

The Seven Founders of the Servites

February 12

GOD SPEAKS TO US

This child [Jesus] is... like a sign which shall be contradicted; and [Mary]thy own soul a sword shall pierce.
—Cf. Luke 2:34-35

MEDITATION

In the 13th century, when the most flourishing parts of Italy were torn apart by the schism of Frederick II and by cruel factions, Divine Providence raised up many saints, among whom were seven noblemen of Florence in Tuscany. Far from becoming involved with ongoing rivalries, they met regularly to pray and to encourage each other to progress in the practice of the Christian virtues.

Now, on August 15, 1233, while they were praying, the Blessed Virgin appeared to them and invited them to embrace a more perfect kind of life. The following September 8, after consulting the Bishop of Florence, they began their new life, once they had sold their property. Wearing a hair shirt under worn clothing, they retired to the countryside to a humble dwelling. Their leader, Bonfilio Monaldi, died in 1262.

The specific charism of the Order of Servites is meditation on the Passion of Jesus and the sorrows of Our Lady: the announcement by the old man Simeon of the sword that would pierce her heart, the flight to Egypt, the loss of the Child Jesus in the Temple, the meeting with Jesus during his ascent to Calvary, the death of her Son on the cross, His descent from the cross and His burial in the tomb. The Servites spread the scapular of Our Lady of Sorrows to promote the devotion of the faithful to the sufferings of the Blessed Virgin.

May the contemplation of Our Lady's sorrows help us to understand that Jesus is indeed a sign of contradiction, as

Simeon predicted. Consequently, the world is divided into two camps. There are those who love Jesus, and those who want nothing to do with Him. So let us promise Him that we will remain faithful. To achieve this we must avoid the trap of seeking a way to reconcile the demands of religion with the attractions of the world. We must choose sides if we do not want to lose our way on the slippery slope of mediocrity. God loves upright souls, sincere souls, determined souls, who know what they want and consistently live in complete conformity with the Faith.

O my Jesus, help me to be a well-adjusted Catholic, proud of my faith, so that I may console You and cooperate in the salvation of souls.

Attributes

The Seven Holy Founders of the Order of Servites are depicted kneeling before an image of Our Lady of the Seven Sorrows.

Prayer

O Lord Jesus Christ, Who, to honor the memory of the sorrows of Thy most holy Mother, didst through seven blessed Fathers enrich Thy Church with a new family of her Servants: mercifully grant that we may be so linked in fellowship to them in their sorrows, as to share also in their joys. (Collect)

Thoughts

- "O all ye that pass by the way, attend, and see if there be any sorrow like to my sorrow."

    —Lamentations 1:12

- "Forget not the groanings of thy mother."

    —Sirach 7:29

Resolutions

1 Pray the *Stabat mater* attentively. (See appendix.)

2 Meditate for 10 minutes on the seven sorrows of Our Lady.

3 Dust off your crucifixes and other devotional articles.

St. Catherine de Ricci

February 13

God speaks to us

But God forbid that I should glory, save in the cross of our Lord Jesus Christ; by whom the world is crucified to me, and I to the world.

—Galatians 6:14

Meditation

Catherine de Ricci (1522-1590), born in Florence (Italy), showed a profound piety during her childhood. From the age of three years, she practiced prayer and sought silence so as to live as much as possible in the presence of God. Raised in a monastery of the Dominican Order, she soon had a special devotion to the Passion of Our Lord. She loved to pray daily before a statue of Christ on the cross. At the age of 13, she received the habit of the Third Order at the cloistered monastery of Prato (Tuscany).

One of her characteristic virtues was the delicate way in which she practiced fraternal correction. To encourage her in her virtues, Our Lord made her enjoy ecstasies, raptures, and visions. One day He gave her a ring and imprinted the marks of His Passion on her hands, feet, and side. For several years, on Thursdays and Fridays, she endured the torments of Jesus in His Passion.

She also had a great devotion to the souls in purgatory. Thus, she agreed to take upon herself the sufferings of one of them. "God answered her prayer so thoroughly that we saw her flesh swell, sparks come out of it, and her tongue turn black like coal. The sisters could not hold her hand; even her cell was ablaze with her burning breath."[27] Renowned for her gift of prophetic lights, she knew the feelings of bitterness or the other temptations of her sisters. As the superior of her community, she demonstrated great prudence and profound humility, carrying out the most laborious

---

[27] Père Cormier, *Une année avec les saints*, Le Sel, 2008, p. 44.

St. Catherine de Ricci

responsibilities while being very self-effacing. Having learned that the sisters had written down the graces with which she was favored, she hastened to burn these documents. Weakened by illness, she received extreme unction before joining her Divine Bridegroom in heaven. Her last prayer was the *Our Father*. The convent then resounded with the harmonious song of the angels: Jesus led His glorious bride in triumph.

Invocation

St. Catherine is invoked to endure physical pains.

Prayer

O Lord Jesus Christ, Who wast pleased that Blessed Catherine, Thy Virgin, should be inflamed with Thy love and made illustrious by the contemplation of Thy Passion, grant through her intercession that, devoutly dwelling on the mysteries of the Passion, we may merit to receive its fruits. (Collect)

Thoughts

- "May the uncertainty of our perseverance in good keep us in the humility and esteem of our neighbor!"
  —St. Catherine de Ricci, *AS*, p. 44

- "The practice of prayer for the deliverance of souls from purgatory is the most agreeable to God, after prayer for the conversion of sinners."
  —The Curé of Ars, *PPJ2*, November 23

Resolutions

1 Recite a prayer for the relief of a soul in purgatory.
2 Be tactful with family members who are temperamental.
3 Perform a service at home to make common life easier. Vacuum, wash the car, straighten your room…

St. Valentine

February 14

GOD SPEAKS TO US

If any man will come after Me, let him deny himself, and take up his cross, and follow Me.
—Communion: Matthew 16:24

MEDITATION

Valentine († ca. 270), a priest, was virtuous to such a degree that his reputation soon spread to the whole city of Rome. Learning that he was Christian, Emperor Claudius II had Valentine arrested. At first, he tried to approach Valentine, offering him his friendship, but Valentine took the opportunity to testify clearly to his faith in Jesus Christ and even invited the Emperor to reject idols.

Impressed by Valentine's words and by the virtues emanating from him, Claudius II seemed to have the desire to learn religion, but the prefect of the city, Calpurnius, proclaimed loudly and clearly that it was out of the question to abandon the gods they believed in.

The Emperor feared a rebellion if he sided with Valentine. He yielded to his underling and delivered Valentine into the hands of Judge Asterius to punish him for sacrilege. Hearing Valentine speak of Our Lord, Asterius was intrigued and touched, and said to him essentially, "How are you sure that Jesus Christ is the true light? If that is the case, let him give sight to my adopted daughter who has been blind for two years. Then, if He heals her, I will believe." Valentine took him at his word. He had them bring the girl and addressed this prayer to God: "Lord Jesus Christ, You are the true light; enlighten this child." No sooner had he finished his exhortation than the girl was cured. Touched by grace, Asterius and his wife converted. The saint ordered them to break their idols; he also asked them to fast for three days and to forgive those who had offended them; then he baptized them along with the other members of their family.

St. Valentine

The Emperor, still fearing reprisals if he condoned this radical change by one of his most prominent subordinates, ordered that Asterius be put to death, as well as those who had been baptized with him.

As for Valentine, after a long stay in prison, he was beaten with gnarled sticks and then beheaded on the Flaminian Way, between Rome and Terni.

Invocation and Patronage

St. Valentine is invoked for the healing of epileptics. He is the patron of fiancés and of beekeepers.

Prayer

Grant, we beseech Thee, O almighty God, that we, who celebrate the heavenly birthday of blessed Valentine, Thy Martyr, may by his intercession be delivered from all the evils that threaten us. (Collect)

Thoughts

- "What is the life of the saints, if not the Gospel put into action? There is no more difference between the written Gospel and the life of the saints than there is between notated music and sung music."
  —St. Francis de Sales, *PPJ*, January 25

- "Courage! Do we not have the opportunity to believe that our Savior loves us? Yes, certainly we have it; and why do we worry about temptations?"
  —St. Francis de Sales, *PPJ*, March 1

Resolutions

1. Pray a decade of the Rosary to ask for the conversion of the Jews and the Muslims.
2. Edify your neighbor by irreproachable conduct.
3. Honor to the Catholic Church by witnessing that it alone holds the truth.

Saints Faustinus and Jovita

February 15

GOD SPEAKS TO US

But the salvation of the just is from the Lord, and He is their protector in the time of trouble.

—Introit: Psalm 36:39

MEDITATION

While the names of the notables who lived in Brescia, Lombardy (Italy) at the beginning of the second century are hardly remembered, the Church has preserved the memory of two great saints of this region, Faustinus and Jovita. The whole world sings the praise of the heroic virtues of these two blood brothers, of whom the first was a priest and the second a deacon under the Emperors Trajan and Hadrian.

They were the first to be denounced to the public authorities because of their zeal in proclaiming Jesus Christ. By their preaching they had led pagans to renounce the false gods and to be baptized.

The two brothers were taken to the temple of the sun in front of a gleaming statue of this false god surrounded by rays of gold, but the moment they started to pray, it was covered with soot. The Emperor then commanded them to clean it, but as soon as they touched it, it crumbled into ashes. After that, the Emperor, infuriated, subjected them to various tortures, but the Good Lord did not permit them to feel pain. For example, they were condemned to be devoured by wild animals, but the beasts lay down at their feet. However, they then endured great sufferings, subjected to the cruelest hunger and the most burning thirst, but angels gave them strength. It was then decided to burn them alive, but when they approached the flames died out. When thrown into the sea, they were delivered by divine force. Finally, they were decapitated around the year 120.

Saints Faustinus and Jovita

"When we compare our trials with yours, noble martyrs of Christ, and our combats with those that you had to fight, how grateful ought we to be to our Lord for having so mercifully taken our weakness into account! Should we have been able to endure the tortures, wherewith you had to purchase heaven, we that are so easily led to break the law of God, so tardy in our conversion, so weak in faith and charity? And yet, we are made for that same heaven which you now possess. God holds out a crown to us also, and we are not at liberty to refuse it. Rouse up our courage, brave martyrs! Obtain for us a spirit of resistance against the world and our evil inclinations; that thus we may confess our Lord Jesus Christ, not only with our lips, but with our works too, and testify, by our conduct, that we are Christians."[28]

Prayer

O God, Who dost gladden us by the annual feast of Thy holy Martyrs Faustinus and Jovita, mercifully grant that we who rejoice in their merits may be inspired by their example. (Collect)

Thoughts

- "For patience is necessary for you; that, doing the will of God, you may receive the promise."

  —Hebrews 10:36

- "So many bitter trials, so many proofs of love."

  —Padre Pio, *PPJ*, October 6

Resolutions

1 Pray the Fifth Sorrowful Mystery for present-day martyrs.

2 Pray the act of charity often to increase your union with God.

3 Agree to follow Jesus Christ by bearing your cross day by day.

---

[28] Guéranger, Dom Prosper. *The Liturgical Year: Septuagesima*, trans. Dom Laurence Shepherd (Great Falls, MT: St. Bonaventure Publications, 2000), 4th edition, vol. 4, pp. 277-278.

St. Juliana of Nicomedia

February 16

GOD SPEAKS TO US

The wicked have waited for me to destroy me: but I have understood Thy testimonies.

—Introit: Psalm 118:95

MEDITATION

Juliana († ca. 307), born at Cumea in Italy, despite her pagan parents, had the happiness of being Christian. A young man named Eleusius, of a noble family, wished to take her for his wife, but she refused vehemently. She let him know that she was a Christian and that it was out of the question for her to marry a pagan. After the young man revealed to Juliana's father the religion of his daughter, she suffered a whipping and prison. Then, Juliana's father put her into the hands of her suitor, who had become prefect of the city. But Juliana stood firm. She gave in neither to flattery nor to threats and clearly stated that she would not change her mind, even if she had to suffer terribly.

Eleusius, furious, multiplied the most painful abuses against his innocent victim. Juliana was whipped, hung by her hair, burned with flaming torches and red-hot irons, but she remained faithful. At that moment, the devil, disguising himself as an angel of light, appeared to her and told her that she had suffered enough and that she could now obey the Emperor and sacrifice to the gods. The saint understood, of course, that such advice did not come from the Holy Ghost; so, she paid it no heed. She prayed to God to strengthen her so that she could endure new torments, if that was His will. Then she heard a voice from heaven saying: "Juliana, have courage, I am with you." Instantly she found herself healed of her wounds, and free. When she got up from the ground, she saw a devil near her. She bound him up with the chain that had served as her bond and treated him like a slave.

After that, she was again summoned to court. The prefect Eleusius found her more beautiful than ever, but unable to satisfy his passion, he decided to make her suffer new torments. The young woman was plunged into a cauldron of molten lead without being harmed. This impressed the witnesses so much that 500 people converted on the spot. A cauldron of boiling oil also left her unscathed, so to put an end to his victim, the judge had her beheaded.

Attribute and Invocation

The attribute of St. Juliana is a chained devil. She is invoked against contagious diseases.

Prayer

May blessed Juliana, Thy Virgin and Martyr, we beseech Thee, O Lord, obtain pardon for us: for she merited Thy constant good pleasure by her life of chastity, attributed by her to Thy power. (Collect)

Thoughts

- "Do not be afraid of all the pitfalls that the devil has for you: the Lord is always with you. He will fight with you."

  —Padre Pio, *PPJ*, January 10

- "If you are insulted, bear it with patience: it is the mark of true humility."

  —St. Alphonsus de Liguori, *SJJ*, p. 199

Resolutions

1 Pray the First Joyful Mystery for the young people among your acquaintances that they will not make plans to marry frivolously.

2 Read the rules for the discernment of spirits by St. Ignatius of Loyola to avoid the snares of the devil.

3 Examine your conscience for a better knowledge of your faults, especially on the occasions when they are manifested.

Blessed Henry Suso

February 17

GOD SPEAKS TO US

That I may know Him ... being made conformable to His death, if by any means I may attain to the resurrection which is from the dead.

—Epistle: Philippians 3:10-11

MEDITATION

Henry Suso (ca. 1295-1366) would illuminate the Rhine countries during the late Middle Ages by his holiness and teaching. He was born in Germany near Lake Constance of a frail and sensitive mother, to whom he became very close, and of a self-indulgent father who would repel Henry by his brusqueness. He was delicate by nature, and very early his life was marked by suffering.

He entered the Dominicans at the age of 14. Very quickly, he seemed to flourish there, even though later on he blamed himself for spending his novitiate years in lukewarmness, even in dissipation. He felt an ardent need to love and did not find in creatures anything to satisfy his aspirations. But soon, he let himself be touched by the sufferings of Jesus in His Passion. This led him not only to meditation, but also to imitation of his Beloved. He experienced the wisdom of the cross.

He sought silence and solitude. For ten years he led a secluded life, his cell serving as both a prison and a refuge. The hours of grace in which he was filled with God were especially the ones between matins and Mass. When he celebrated Mass, all he had to do was pronounce the *Sursum corda* ["Let us lift up our hearts"] of the Preface, and those who were attending felt driven to pray fervently. A witness reported that he saw him lit up with an inner flame, as if he had become lost in God. His contemplation of the Passion led him to great mortifications and penances: hunger, thirst, a bed made of a plank covered with a mat, an iron chain around his waist, a cross bristling with nails between his shoulder blades. During these years of retreat, he composed most of his writings, notably the *Book of the Eternal Wisdom.*

Having arrived at the age of 40, he left the cloistered life to devote himself to apostolic ministry in a land ravaged by war and the Black Plague. He went in search of the lost sheep and showed his zeal in ministering to fervent nuns. One of them, Sister Elsbeth, his spiritual daughter, later recorded his life. He shone with his charity and by a mysterious influence which emanated from his whole person when he spoke and when he prayed. He made Catholic doctrine easy to understand and pleasing to hear. His final years were bathed in a serene light. Pope Gregory XVI enrolled him in the ranks of the blessed.

Prayer

O God, who hast made Blessed Henry, Thy Confessor, admirable by his corporal mortification and by his charity, grant that we may show forth Christ crucified in our deeds and live with Him in our hearts.

—Dominican Rite Collect

Thoughts

- "Free yourself from all that can bring you difficulty, attachments, and worry."

   —Blessed Henry Suso, *LS*, 2:180

- "A man whose spirit is stripped of all that concerns the creature will contemplate the divine glory of the heavenly Lord, the Divine Wisdom, and will be transformed into the same image, from glory into glory, from the glory of His tender humanity to the clarity of His eternal divinity."

   —Blessed Henry Suso, *GLL*, 4:111-112

Resolutions

1. Search for silence in order to live closer to God. Turn off your cell phone during the day.

2. Break off dangerous attachments to creatures.

3. Have an image of Jesus on the cross so as to honor Him regularly and to remember the sufferings that He endured for us.

St. Bernadette

February 18

GOD SPEAKS TO US

Hearken, O daughter, and see, and incline thy ear: and forget thy people and thy father's house.

—Psalm 44:11

MEDITATION

Bernadette (1844-1879) was the masterpiece of Our Lady. She was born in the Diocese of Tarbes, where devotion to the Blessed Virgin was particularly held in honor. In her family God was the first to be served. They suffered together, they prayed together, they loved each other deeply. They heard neither complaints nor murmuring despite the poverty of the house, a former dungeon. Bernadette saw her father jailed for eight days for having taken a board of abandoned wood. When he returned, he did not complain in the least about this blatant injustice. Beyond misery and humiliation, very early on Bernadette experienced suffering. She had asthma from the age of six and contracted cholera at the age of 11. This is how the Blessed Virgin fashioned her masterpiece!

Bernadette seemed to have been preserved from voluntary actual sin. Her purity facilitated her elevation to God. She discovered the Creator's goodness in nature on the hills of Bartrès. Her striving for God was manifested in her desire for catechism and for Holy Communion. She had a thirst for God. The Queen of Heaven would quench it by appearing to her eighteen times, revealing secrets and messages.

By making a beautiful sign of the cross, Bernadette evoked the mystery of the Trinity and that of the Redemption. The more Bernadette looked at the Immaculate, the more she came into intimate contact with God. This contemplation made it easy for her to do the penance she showed by kissing the earth, washing herself in muddy water, and eating grass during an apparition at Our Lady's orders. Her love of God also gave her the strength to face the priest, Fr. Peyramale, who treated her unsympathetically at the beginning of the apparitions. Always true to herself, she did not let herself be influenced by popularity or hostility.

However, after the apparitions the Blessed Virgin had not yet finished her teaching mission. She would make Bernadette participate in her own self-effacement in the convent in Nevers (1866-1879), where she would live a hidden life under a Mother Superior who was rather harsh towards her. She would also make Bernadette take part, after her example, in the Passion and Cross of her Son. By introducing her into her intimacy, Our Lady made Bernadette share in her hatred of sin and her love for sinners. Bernadette did penance and suffered for them. To pray and to suffer, that was her whole life.

St. Bernadette, intercede for me, that I may go to the school of Our Lady so as to be united to Jesus, and that I may one day become worthy of happiness in heaven.

Prayer

O God, protector and friend of the humble, Who filled Thy servant, Bernadette, with joy by the apparition and the conversation of the Immaculate Virgin Mary: grant, we pray, that by the simple way of faith we may be counted worthy to see Thee face to face in heaven. (Collect)

Thoughts

- "Love humility. Love to believe that you are nothing before God. God will then fill your heart. Flee from praise. God alone is good, the Gospel tells us."
  —St. Bernadette, *PPJ*, March 15

- "Jesus, Jesus, I no longer feel my cross when I think of yours."
  —St. Bernadette, *PPJ*, May 8

Resolutions

1 Make the sign of the cross correctly.

2 Avoid showing off to others.

3 Be content with your lot and, consequently, do not complain about anything.

St. Margaret of Cortona

February 19 (celebrated on February 22)

GOD SPEAKS TO US

For as it was your mind to go astray from God; so when you return again you shall seek him ten times as much.
—Baruch 4:28

MEDITATION

Among the saints in Paradise, some have been faithful to God from the cradle to the grave while others have failed seriously, at least for some time. We admire the first group, but naturally those in the second seem to us more accessible.

In this second category, we can mention Margaret of Cortona (1247-1297). She was born in Umbria (Italy) to a family of modest means. Her mother died when she was only seven years old. From then on, neglected by her family, very beautiful physically, she let others lead her down the enchanting path of worldly pleasures. At the age of adolescence, she made the acquaintance of a gentleman. She had a sinful relationship with him for nine years, until she was 26. The violent death of her murdered seducer put an end to her disordered conduct, and she atoned for it during the last 23 years of her life with such zeal that Pope Benedict XIII would compare her to St. Mary Magdalene.

She acknowledged her sins and from then on declared war on her body, saying: "You defeated me; I will defeat you!" These were not empty words. One day, to atone for her sins through humiliation, she went to her parish church and after Mass, she knelt before a lady, saying aloud, "Here at your feet is this infamous sinner who has disgraced her family and her country: forgive me my transgressions." After three years of purification, she took the habit of the Third Order of St. Francis. She then led a very mortified life, condemned herself to eat extremely frugal meals, to lie on the bare ground, and she chastised her flesh with rough hair shirts and bloody scourgings. Her life was enriched by visions and the gift of miracles, but also punctuated by dark nights. There are few souls to whom God gave the grace of a transformation as rapid and as complete as St. Margaret's. One day, Our Lord told her the reason: "I have destined you to be the net of fishermen. I want you to be the light of those who sit in the darkness of vice; I want the example of your conversion to preach hope to sinners; finally I want future centuries to be convinced that I am always ready to open the arms of My mercy to the prodigal child who sincerely returns to Me."

Invocation

St. Margaret is invoked by women seeking to have children.

Prayer

I ask nothing but to love you always, and to serve you without ever offending your divine majesty.

—St. Margaret of Cortona, *Au. S.*, 1:478

Thoughts

- "He is a chosen one, who has his heart detached from all earthly covetousness, is united to his Creator, constantly tends toward Him, and yearns for Him alone."
  —St. Margaret of Cortona, *ACP*, vol. XV, p. 88

- "How many persons restored to life, Lord Jesus! How many poor sinners have You called to yourself! Heaven is full of them. It is the exquisite fruit of Your painful Passion."

  —Père D.-A. Mortier, *E*, p. 399

Resolutions

1 Recite an act of contrition from the depths of your heart.

2 Make reparation for the disorders of your past life by striving to be an example for those around you.

3 Declare war on your predominant fault.

Jacinta of Fatima

February 20

GOD SPEAKS TO US

Jesus said to his disciples: Suffer the little children to come unto me.

—Mark 10:14

MEDITATION

Jacinta Marto was born on March 11, 1910, at Aljustrel, near Fatima (Portugal). She was baptized there eight days later. As a young shepherd, she loved to take the little white sheep on her knees. She was by nature emotional and affectionate; she loved to sing and was very fond of dancing.

In 1916, with her brother Francisco and her cousin Lucia, she received the visit of an angel. He taught them prayers and prepared them spiritually to receive the confidences of Our Lady the following year. The Blessed Virgin appeared to them on the 13th of each month, from May to October 1917, except for the month of August, when the visit of the heavenly mother took place on the 19th, since the children were in prison on the 13th. Our Lady asked them to pray the Rosary every day and promised to lead them to heaven. In the month of July, Jacinta was very impressed by the vision of hell and especially by the fact that it is eternal, which led her to multiply her sacrifices for the conversion of sinners. For example, she stopped dancing, she gave food intended for her to poor children, she deprived herself of drink, she tied a cord around her waist, and beat her legs with nettles. Though she was still a child, she had a profound interior life. Her cousin noticed: "What I felt with Jacinta," she said, "is what we usually feel around a holy person, who seems to communicate with God in everything. Jacinta always had a serious, modest, and amiable demeanor, which seemed to testify to the presence of God in all her actions, which is usually typical of highly virtuous persons already advanced in age."[29] If in her presence, someone took

---

[29] *Memoires de Soeur Lucie* (Téqui, 1991), 190.

the liberty of saying or doing something inappropriate, she did not hesitate to reproach him and say: "Do not do that, you offend Our Lord, and He is already so much offended."[30] Jacinta made her first communion in the Spring of 1918 and fell ill in December. Here again she offered her sufferings for the conversion of sinners. A victim of the Spanish flu, she died, all alone, after a last visit of Our Lady, on February 20, 1920, at the hospital *Dona Estefania* in Lisbon.

Prayer

Most Holy Trinity—Father, Son, and Holy Spirit—I adore Thee profoundly. I offer Thee the most precious Body, Blood, Soul, and Divinity of Jesus Christ, present in all the tabernacles of the world, in reparation for the outrages, sacrileges, and indifferences whereby He is offended. And through the infinite merits of His Most Sacred Heart and the Immaculate Heart of Mary, I beg of Thee the conversion of poor sinners.

—Prayer taught by the Angel of Portugal

Thoughts

- "There will appear fashions that will greatly offend Our Lord."

—Jacinta

- "I will suffer for the love of Our Lord, to make reparation for the insults against the Immaculate Heart of Mary, for the conversion of sinners, and for the Holy Father."

—Jacinta, *MSL*, pp. 44-45

Resolutions

1 Draw inspiration from Jacinta's vision of hell to guard against it and to convince skeptics that it exists.

2 Examine honestly before God (and a mirror) the way you dress.

3 Make a sacrifice to beg for the conversion of a sinner.

---

[30] *Ibid.*, 191.

Blessed Noël Pinot

February 21

God speaks to us

If the world hate you, know ye, that it hath hated Me before you.

—John 15:18

Meditation

Noël Pinot was born on December 19, 1747, in Angers into a family of deeply Christian workers; he was the youngest of sixteen children. When raised to the priesthood, he had no other ambition but to consecrate his life to God and to sacrifice it in the service of the souls that would be entrusted to him.

At first a vicar of two different parishes for nine years, he became chaplain to the hospice for incurables in Angers for 15 years. At the age of 40, in 1788, he was promoted to assistant priest of the parish of Louroux-Béconnais, the largest in the Diocese of Angers. Apart from the times of prayer, his life was divided among the pulpit, the confessional, catechism classes, sick calls, and care of the poor. When he gave away all the clothes he could buy for others, he deprived himself, keeping only the bare minimum. The habitual thought of God's presence kept him far from evil and made him capable of all sorts of good deeds. His constant concern was to raise his life to the height of his priestly dignity. His Mass was a real sermon for those who attended.

Thus the glory of martyrdom would be the reward for the priestly virtues that he practiced to a heroic degree.

After having spent himself for his flock, he would lay down his life for his faith. He emphatically rejected the Civil Constitution of the Clergy on July 12, 1790. The mayor declared him dismissed from his office. But he protested: "I remain," he said, "the lawful Curé of Louroux." Denounced by the city council, he was arrested on March 5, 1791, and treated as a provocateur, as a conspirator, as seditious. He was then exiled from his parish for two years. He continued nonetheless his priestly ministry as far as prudence allowed. But in 1793, anti-religious passions reached their climax. The Vendée arose. During the period when the region of Angers was liberated, he returned from his exile, but soon the Reign of Terror began. Noël Pinot, reduced to hiding, was discovered on February 9, 1794. He was then overwhelmed with insults and ill-treatment. The Military Commission pronounced his death sentence. In mockery, it was suggested that he put on his priestly vestments.

Thus vested, he mounted the scaffold on February 21, at 3:00 p.m. Raising his eyes to heaven, he exclaimed: "*Introibo ad altare Dei*; I will go in to the altar of God." This was how he paid for his inviolable attachment to Jesus Christ and His Holy Church.

Prayer

O God, who hast filled Thy martyr Noël Pinot with zeal for the salvation of souls and with an admirable constancy in the faith, may we, by his intercession and his example, merit to be found firm in the faith and faithful until death. (Collect)

Thoughts

- "There are two types of martyr, one in secret, the other in public. Even if the persecution does not appear outwardly, the merit of martyrdom exists in secret when the soul is ready to suffer and it burns with ardent courage."

  —St. Gregory the Great, *PPJ*, August 5

- "Martyrdom is the sacrifice that man makes to God of his life and the Mass is the sacrifice that God makes to man of His body and His blood."

  —The Curé of Ars, *MR*, p. 159

RESOLUTIONS

1. Pray the Fourth Sorrowful Mystery to ask God for the grace of fidelity to your commitments: marriage, work, and so forth.

2. Attend Mass with devotion by thinking of Calvary.

3. Cultivate your Eucharistic devotion by reading the prayers that precede Communion and by having an irreproachable attitude.

The Chair of St. Peter

February 22

God speaks to us

Thou art Peter; and upon this rock I will build My Church, and the gates of hell shall not prevail against it.

—Matthew 16:18

Meditation

The feast of the Chair of St. Peter was instituted to commemorate the preaching of the head of the Apostles in Antioch, the metropolitan city of the East. He established his episcopal see there before settling in Rome, and this was the diocese where for the first time the faithful were called by the name of *Christians* (Acts 11:26). Our Lord called 12 Apostles and chose Peter as their leader. St. Matthew, while listing the names of the 12, specified: "the first was Simon called Peter" (Mt. 10:2). St. Mark added that Our Lord "gave to Simon the name Peter" (Mk. 3:16) in order to prepare him for his future mission as head of the Church.

Peter exercised this primacy "beginning in Jerusalem," according to the words of Our Lord Himself (Lk. 24:47), then in Antioch, and finally in Rome. The primacy of Peter lives on in his successors; over the centuries the popes would enjoy a primacy in the exercise of their office. The Chair symbolizes the primacy of Peter and of his successors in teaching. It is, in fact, a divinely revealed dogma that when the Roman Pontiff, in fulfilling the office of the teacher of all Christians, defines by virtue of his supreme apostolic authority that a doctrine on faith and morals must be held true by the Universal Church, he enjoys fully, through the divine assistance promised to him in the person of St. Peter, the privilege of infallibility, hence the expression *ex cathedra* which manifests that a pope enjoys infallibility when he defines certain truths. For example, when Pope Pius XII defined the dogma of the Assumption of the Blessed Virgin, that is, her triumphal ascent to heaven, body and soul, he enjoyed that privilege. Henceforth, this definition is unchangeable.

Since Divine Revelation was concluded at the death of the last apostles, we can no longer expect any new revelations. Indeed, Vatican Council I tells us that "the Holy Ghost was not promised to the successors of Peter that they might disclose a new doctrine, but rather that they might reverently guard and faithfully explain the deposit of the Faith."[31] The pope simply has the power to draw from the treasure of Revelation in order to make certain implicit truths explicit, in order to expound them and defend them against errors; hence the dogmas of faith defined down the centuries.

The relics of the chair of Peter are preserved in the Basilica of St. Peter in Rome.

Prayer

O God, Who by delivering to Thy blessed Apostle Peter the keys of the kingdom of heaven, didst confer upon him the pontifical power of binding and of loosing, grant that, by the help of his intercession, we may be freed from the bonds of sin. (Collect)

Thoughts

- Love the Church, since the Church loves you so much.
  —St. Augustine

- No one can have God for a Father, if he does not have the Church for his Mother.
  —St. Cyprian, *UE*, ch. 4

Resolutions

1 Pray the First Glorious Mystery that the Pope, even and above all in the 21st century, may fully proclaim Catholic faith and morals and defend them against their enemies.

2 Defend the Church when she is attacked.

3 In all circumstances, behave in a manner worthy of our nature as children of God and of the Church.

---

[31] Vatican Council I, Session IV, chapter 4; Denzinger-Hünermann, n. 3070.

St. Peter Damian

February 23

God speaks to us

The zeal of thy house hath eaten me up.

—John 2:17

Meditation

Born in Ravenna (Italy) to a poor and large family, Peter Damian (988-1072) was at first abandoned by his parents to the point that he found himself on the street, half dead. A charitable soul cared for him and gave him back to his parents, who from then on would take care of him more attentively. However, they died shortly thereafter. The young child was then taken in by one of his brothers, but very quickly he was treated like a slave.

In this miserable state, he did not withdraw into himself, but instead showed signs of holy dispositions. Once he found a coin. Rather than take the opportunity to buy treats, he had Masses celebrated for the repose of his father's soul. Soon, another of his brothers, by the name of Damian, archpriest of Ravenna, took pity on him and paid for his education. As a sign of gratitude, Peter added his brother's first name to his own.

From that time on, he demonstrated the utmost mortification of the senses. He wore a hair shirt and fasted frequently. One day, when he was tempted to commit a sin of impurity, he plunged into an icy pond to extinguish the fire of concupiscence. Soon he decided to abandon the world to give himself totally to God in the monastic life of the Camaldolese Order. He thus prepared himself to undertake his work of restoring Holy Church, which had been brought low by the moral disorders of his times. His reputation for sanctity led Pope Stephen X to create him a cardinal and Bishop of Ostia, functions which he later abandoned so as to return to his solitary life. He was a proponent of the Friday fast, in honor of the Cross of Our Lord, and of venerating the Blessed Virgin on Saturdays.

After a life resplendent with virtues, his soul flew towards the Divine Master whom he loved so much. In this season of the liturgical year, he invites us to conversion.

O St. Peter Damian, you were an example of penance in the midst of a corrupt century; come to our aid. Today as never before, Satan seeks to debase souls by plunging them into the vices of pride, selfishness, and impurity. Revive in our souls the memory of the sorrowful Passion of Jesus so as to excite in us repentance and to strengthen our virtue of hope.

Attributes and invocation

St. Peter Damian is depicted as a hermit, with the cardinal's hat beside him, or else as a penitent with a discipline. He is invoked against headaches.

Prayer

Grant unto us, we beseech Thee, O almighty God, so to follow the counsels and example of blessed Peter, Thy Confessor and Bishop, that we may, by despising earthly things, obtain everlasting joys. (Collect)

Thoughts

- "The soul [of the just man] is a paradise; it is a garden of delights where God makes His dwelling."
  —St. Peter Damian, *PL* 144, 269c

- "If fasting for one day is good, fasting for two or three days is better."
  —St. Peter Damian, *Lettres,* VI, 27, 417c

Resolutions

1 Meditate for 10 minutes on two or three stations of the Way of the Cross.

2 Have a Mass celebrated for a deceased loved one, or attend a Mass and pray for this intention.

3 On Fridays, make a sacrifice during a meal.

St. Matthias

February 24

God speaks to us

You, who have followed me, [says Jesus] … you also shall sit on 12 seats judging the 12 tribes of Israel.
—Communion: St. Matthew 19:28

Meditation

Our Lord chose 12 Apostles to extend His kingdom in souls. One among them, Judas, was unfaithful to God; he went so far as to deliver his Divine Master to the high priests for 30 pieces of silver. Consumed with remorse and prey to despair, he threw the money away and finally hanged himself. In order to maintain the number of evangelical laborers chosen by Jesus, between the Ascension and Pentecost, the apostles cast lots to name the one who would replace the betrayer. Of the two selected from among the 72 disciples who had followed Christ throughout His ministry, the lot fell to Matthias. David had prophesied the betrayal by Judas and his replacement by another disciple.[32] We have very little information about the life of the new apostle. We know merely that he evangelized Judea and suffered martyrdom: he was stoned and then beheaded by the blow of an ax.

This feast of St. Matthias, in recalling the betrayal of Judas, is an invitation for us to ask God for the grace of perseverance in our state of life and for fidelity to our mission as baptized persons. Whatever our degree of virtue may be, we remain fragile. St. Paul says that "God … hath shined in our hearts … but we have this treasure in earthen vessels." (II Cor. 4:6-7). It is an invitation to have humble opinions of ourselves. St. Matthias shows us what man is capable of under the action of the Holy Ghost, so let us beg him to intercede for us with Jesus.

"Apostle Matthias, you completed the College of Apostles after the fall of Judas; the heavenly splendor of your wise

---

[32] Psalm 108

discourses has dispelled the darkness of idolatry, by the virtue of the Holy Ghost: now pray to the Lord to grant peace to our souls and His great mercy."[33]

Attributes and patronage

When he is depicted in the group of the apostles, St. Matthias has an ax as his attribute. Alone, he holds a cross with a long shaft. He is the patron of carpenters and of toolmakers.

Prayer

O God, Who didst join blessed Matthias to the company of Thine Apostles, grant, we beseech Thee, that through his intercession, we may ever be conscious of Thy compassion and loving kindness towards us. (Collect)

Thoughts

- "We must admire what is before our eyes, for the visible works of God lift us up to the invisible things, and lead us to contemplate the Creator's infinite majesty, power, wisdom, and goodness."
  —St. Matthias, quoted by Clement of Alexandria

- "We must fight against the flesh and make us of it without flattering it with sinful satisfactions; as for the soul, we must develop it by faith by understanding."
  —St. Matthias, quoted by Clement of Alexandria

Resolutions

1. Pray the Fourth Glorious Mystery while thinking especially about the last words of the *Hail Mary* to ask for final perseverance.
2. Invoke the Holy Ghost before making a decision.
3. Acknowledge your faults and ask forgiveness when you have done wrong.

---

[33] Strophes drawn from the Divine Office of the Byzantine Church

Blessed Sebastian of Aparicio

February 25

GOD SPEAKS TO US

Blessed is the rich man that is found without blemish: and that hath not gone after gold nor put his trust in money nor in treasures.

—Ecclesiasticus 31:8

MEDITATION

Besides the saints listed on the liturgical calendar, there are numerous others confined to the martyrology. Thus for the date of February 25, the Franciscan Order in Spain celebrates Blessed Sebastian of Aparicio (1502-1600).

Born in an honest family in Galicia (Spain), he showed great maturity while still a child.

His purity was severely and repeatedly tested. At the age of 15, he was employed as a domestic servant in the household of a widow, but since it endangered his virtue, he quit. Since similar dangers appeared once again, he made the decision to embark for the New World. At the age of 30, he departed for Mexico, where he settled down as a contractor for public works. He set up large agricultural projects, built roads through previously impenetrable forests, and developed a company that shipped merchandise across Mexico. He acquired considerable revenues and spent them for the benefit of the poor. The Indians themselves were so edified by his conduct that they did not hesitate to offer him their services.

Although he was married twice, Sebastian practiced continence with the consent of his successive wives. Once he was widowed, he found himself suffering from a fatal illness. The physicians felt incapable of curing him. He was at the brink of death. Yet contrary to all expectations, he recovered and decided to end his days in religious life. He entered the

Third Order of St. Francis at the age of 70 and led a very edifying life in it. The friar was distinguished particularly by his kindness, obedience, and poverty in his laborious task of collecting alms, which he performed for 26 years. He was rewarded with extraordinary graces such as knowledge of the future and the ability to read hearts. He had such devotion to the holy angels that they took special care of him. He also had the gift of taming ferocious animals.

Finally, exhausted by the life that he had led and almost a centenarian, he died peacefully in Puebla (Mexico).

O Blessed Sebastian, help me in turn to show magnanimity in fighting against my selfishness so as to make myself useful to my neighbor.

Prayer

Lord, grant that my love for You may not be content with words, but may be proved by generous works.

—Fr. Gabriel, *ID*, vol. VI, p. 186.

Or

Grant, O Lord, … that I may vigilantly control my nature, cooperate with grace, keep Your law, and merit salvation.

—Clement XI, Universal Prayer

Thoughts

- "It is necessary to move from emotional love (*l'amour affectif*) to practical love (*l'amour effectif*), which is the performance of works of charity and the service of the poor, undertaken joyfully, constantly, and lovingly."
  —St. Vincent de Paul, *PPJ*, July 9

- "What good would it do to give aid to the poor, if the motive for this action was not love? That was the reason for all the actions of the Blessed Virgin."
  —St. Vincent de Paul, *PPJ*, July 16

Resolutions

1. Donate to an association that defends the Eastern Christians or to some other charity.
2. Give some of your time to a person in need.
3. Flee dangerous occasions of sin so as to keep control over your passions.

St. Porphyry of Gaza

February 26

GOD SPEAKS TO US

Why are you fearful, O ye of little faith?
—St. Matthew 8:26

MEDITATION

Porphyry (353-420), born in Thessalonica (Greece) of very rich and virtuous parents, was raised in the love of God. As a young adult, he spent several years in a monastery, but his superiors decided not to keep him because of his precarious health. A little later he traveled to Palestine. He arrived in Jerusalem half-dead, but miraculously, at Christ's tomb, the Divine Master appeared to him, nailed to the cross, and said to him, indicating the cross: "Receive and keep this wood." At that very instant, he was cured.

Moved by his virtuous example and by his governing abilities, the Patriarch of Jerusalem ordained him a priest at the age of 40. He was put in charge of guarding the wood of the Holy Cross, just as Jesus had predicted. Several years later, he was consecrated a bishop by the Archbishop of Caesarea. He carried out his ministry in Gaza, a city full of idolaters. There he valiantly fought against paganism, destroying the idols, which earned him persecution. However, his ardent zeal and his gentle, considerate charity enabled him to win over hearts and to convert a large number of unbelievers. He received the gift of miracles in abundance, which facilitated his missionary influence! And so, one day when a great drought descended on the region, the unbelievers claimed that he was responsible. Although they prayed before the statue of Marnas, their idol, to bring rain, it was wasted effort. Given their lack of success, and trusting in Divine Providence, St. Porphyry called for a fast and organized night prayers followed by a procession to ask for rain. His prayers were answered immediately. The miracle was so spectacular that a large number of unbelievers converted. On another occasion, while he was at sea, a terrible storm arose. Seized with panic, the captain of the vessel felt unable to avoid shipwreck. Porphyry spoke to him and told him very calmly that the storm would be quieted, provided that he renounce Arianism and become Christian. The pilot was convinced, and immediately the sea was still.

After 25 years in the episcopate, Porphyry could congratulate himself on the fact that the city of Gaza had become entirely Christian. He breathed his last on February 26, 420.

Prayer

[O Jesus,] if the storm arises, I will take refuge in You; I will call on You with all my heart and all the strength of my faith, certain that You will give me the peace and the victory that I would seek in vain far from You.

—Fr. Gabriel, *ID*, vol. I, p. 239.

Thoughts

- "The Lord wants us to learn from experience that our efforts are insufficient without divine help: this is the reason why He leaves us in the storm until we have recourse to Him with full confidence."

  —Fr. Gabriel, *ID*, vol. I, pp. 237-238

- "The interior storm was the lack of faith. And so Our Lord wants to remedy this interior ailment first; the rest will follow afterward, if He sees fit."

  —Fr. Emmanuel, *M*, p. 61

Resolutions

1 Review in your past life several signs of God's special protection so as to strengthen your trust in Him.

2 When in doubt about the Faith, react with determination and call on St. Porphyry to gain discernment and strength.

3 See whether you have any idols: this singer, that movie star, one athlete, another politician, and replace them with devotion to the saints.

St. Gabriel of the Sorrowful Mother

February 27

GOD SPEAKS TO US

O Lord, you have made him little less than the angels, and crowned him with glory and honor.

—Alleluia: Psalm 8:6

MEDITATION

St. Gabriel, whose secular name was Francis Possenti, was born in Assisi (Italy) on March 1, 1838, in a staunchly Catholic family. He lost his mother at the age of four. H is father, a judge by profession, took charge of his education and that of his 12 brothers and sisters, edifying them by his example.

Although inclined to anger, Francis was severely rebuked by his father, so that little by little he managed to control himself. The Brothers of the Christian Schools and later the Jesuit Fathers happily completed this educational work that had been started at home. Francis showed great devotion to Our Lady. However, for a while he let himself go astray on the path of worldly pleasures. He sensed within himself God's call to a vocation, but it was difficult for him to take the step. Several times he fell seriously ill and decided to dedicate himself to God, but as soon as he was cured, the attraction of the world prevented him from carrying out his plans. Finally, he definitively renounced the world during a procession of the holy Icon of Our Lady (attributed to St. Luke). It seemed to him that the Blessed Virgin was staring at him, and he heard these words: "Francis, the world is no longer for you; you must enter religious life." His father, though at first hesitant, ended up giving his approval. Then at the age of 18, he entered the Passionists, where he received the religious name of Gabriel of the Sorrowful Mother. He profoundly enjoyed the benefits of a life dedicated entirely to God. He learned to live in His presence and acted as though after each one of his actions he would have to appear before the Supreme Judge. The chief object of his devotions was Our Lord's Passion. He also developed a great love for Our Lady of the Seven Sorrows. After five years of religious life, before being ordained a priest, he came down with tuberculosis, and the illness carried him off the following year. He received Extreme Unction on February 26, 1862, and was called to the Lord the next day. His last words were: "Jesus, Mary, Joseph."

Invocation and patronage

St. Gabriel of the Sorrowful Mother is invoked against respiratory illnesses, hernias, and childhood diseases. He is the patron saint of seminarians.

Prayer

O God, Thou didst teach Blessed Gabriel to dwell continually upon the sorrows of Thy most sweet Mother, and hast raised him to the glory of holiness and miracles; grant us through his intercession and example, so to share in the mourning of Thy Mother, that we may be saved by her maternal protection. (Collect)

Thoughts

- "When, with a mother's eyes, she beheld the wounds of her Son, what concerned her was not the death of this Son, but rather the salvation of the world."
  —Adapted from St. Ambrose, *L.* 73, n. 110.

- "Mary, who wept over Jesus, wept over us—but in order to cause the resurrection of our souls through her compassion."
  —Louis Soubigou, *CV,* p. 28

RESOLUTIONS

1. Recite a decade of the Rosary in honor of St. Gabriel for the perseverance of seminarians in their vocation.
2. Meditate for 10 minutes on the sufferings that Mary, our good Mother, endured at the foot of the cross to which her dear Son was nailed.
3. Pray for men and women religious who stand at the foot of the cross like the Blessed Virgin and St. John.

Blessed Antonia

February 28

GOD SPEAKS TO US

I am the Lord your God. Be holy because I am holy.
—Leviticus 11:44

MEDITATION

Antonia (1401-1472) was born in Florence into a noble family. From her childhood she gave undeniable signs of virtue. She married at the age of 15, but found herself widowed several years later with a child who would cause her much concern. Her parents hoped that she would remarry, but she firmly refused. Her choice had been made: she wanted to dedicate herself totally to the Good Lord. She entered the Franciscan Third Order Regular as a tertiary, and at this stage of religious life already manifested great fidelity to grace. However, while recognizing the fervor of her community, she aspired to an even more austere life. She confided in St. John of Capistrano, Vicar General of the Observance. The saint was entirely of her opinion and obtained for her Corpus Christi Monastery in Aquila. She settled there with 12 nuns to follow the first Rule of St. Clare. Antonia and the other nuns made their house so fragrant with the perfume of their virtues that soon other aspirants were knocking at their door, to the point where the number in the community reached 100.

The prioress combined profound humility with great patience. She courageously endured various illnesses. The devil multiplied his attacks in vain, appealing to her through various temptations. The saint resisted them thanks to the life of prayer that she led during the day and prolonged during the night.

God rewarded her fidelity by bestowing extraordinary charisms on her. For example, one night when she was in prayer in the church, a globe of fire came to rest on her head and suddenly illumined the place where she was praying. At other times her sisters saw here lifted up from the ground in delightful ecstasy.[34] After making her final recommendations to her sisters and receiving extreme unction, she died a holy death on February 29, 1472.

O Blessed Antonia, seeing the determination with which you sought holiness and led other souls to embrace the way of perfection, I in turn wish to give to God constantly the place that He deserves in my life: Enlighten me, guide me, strengthen me.

Prayer

"Be perfect as your heavenly Father is perfect!" (Mt. 5:48). Lord, I pray You, repeat this sublime invitation very loud and insistently to my poor soul, so that, under the influence of this ideal, it might finally awaken to a greater generosity, to firmer resolutions, to a more complete trust in Your merciful, redemptive, sanctifying work.

—Fr. Gabriel, *ID*, vol. I, p. 25

Thoughts

- "Let us become saints: that way, after living together on earth, we will remain united forever in Paradise."
  —Padre Pio, *GB*, p. 26

- "A soul that lives united to God does only supernatural things, and the most commonplace acts, instead of separating it from Him, on the contrary only bring it closer and closer to Him."
  —Elizabeth of the Trinity, *L*, 309.

Resolutions

1. Meditate for 10 minutes on the graces that God has given to us in the past.
2. Speak to children about the exalted character of the priestly vocation and the religious life.
3. Accept the suffering connected with a recent or difficult bereavement, and offer it to God in a spirit of reparation for your sins.

---

[34] Père Léon, *Vie des saints (…) de saint François*, p. 177.

St. Albinus (Alvin)

March 1

GOD SPEAKS TO US

Here was a great high priest, whose life was acceptable to God. There was not found the like of him in glory, who kept the law of the Most High.

—Gradual: Ecclesiasticus 44:16, 20

MEDITATION

Although the saints led an edifying life, this was not primarily the result of their natural qualities, but rather of the grace of God that they kept alive by living in His presence. Albinus (470-550) was a striking example of this. He was born in a noble family of Armorica-Brittany, in the diocese of Vannes. From his earliest youth, in order to avoid all dissipation, he practiced mortification of the eyes; he lived in the utmost recollection. He opened his eyes only to praise God. Very soon he consecrated himself to God's service and edified his confreres by his piety in his monastery located near Angers. He seemed to be in constant communication with God. That led the religious of his community to elect him as abbot at the age of 35.

After the death of their bishop, the inhabitants of the city of Angers chose him as successor. As much as he tried to slip away, he found that he was compelled to accept this responsibility. For 21 years, he served as bishop with the utmost care. He aided the poor, cared for the sick, and did everything in his power to eradicate vices. God supported his zeal by granting him the gift of miracles. A woman who had enormous debts was in prison. The saint went to visit her. One of the guards who tried to stop him fell down dead at his feet. St. Albinus then took it upon himself to visit the creditors and to ask them to remit the amount of the debt so as to liberate the poor woman. The saint cured many other sick people simply by making the sign of the cross over them, and he delivered possessed persons. He also employed all his zeal to put an end to a custom that allowed incestuous marriages.

O St. Albinus, give us something of your robust piety, your energetic character, and your intense faith, so that with your help we might do the work of God, which is the work of our salvation.

ATTRIBUTES AND INVOCATION

St. Albinus is depicted as a bishop-exorcist, with possessed men at his feet. He is invoked for abdominal complaints, especially colic, and to hasten the end of the terminally ill.

PRAYER

Almighty, eternal God, Who didst choose Blessed Albinus to be a model Christian, monk, and bishop, and at the same time the benefactor of the poor and the unfortunate, grant that, assisted by his help and guided by his example, we might merit to be crowned with him in heaven. Through Jesus Christ our Lord.

—Prayer, *PS*, vol. II, p. 37

THOUGHTS

- "Let us not imagine that our whole interior is empty. Inside of us there is an incomparably sumptuous palace, in a word: one worthy of the Master to whom it belongs."
—St. Teresa of Avila, *Ch P*, chap. 30

- "'The kingdom of God is within you' (Lk. 17:21), the Lord said. Return to God with your whole heart, and abandon this miserable world, and your soul will find rest."
—*The Imitation of Christ*, Book II, chap. 1

RESOLUTIONS

1 Meditate for 10 minutes on the presence of God in your soul and try to think of it again several times during the day.

2 Practice custody of the eyes when you walk down the street so as to preserve more vividly the thought of God present in you.

3 Visit prisoners and pray that judicial errors may be brought to light.

St. Paphnutius

March 2 (celebrated on March 3)

GOD SPEAKS TO US

Judge not, and you shall not be judged. Condemn not, and you shall not be condemned.

—Luke 6:37

MEDITATION

The lives of the Desert Fathers transport us back to the history of another era that is rife with miraculous and sometimes unusual events, as demonstrated by the story of Paphnutius, a fourth-century monk of the Thebaid. One day, while wondering about his degree of union with God, he received an interior light that let him know that he had arrived at the same level of virtue as a nearby wandering musician. Wounded in his self-love and curious to know more, he went in search of that man, who admitted that he was a thief and had done nothing good in his whole life, except in two situations. Once he came to the defense of a consecrated virgin whom two criminals were trying to violate. And on another occasion, having become acquainted with a woman whose husband and children had been imprisoned because of a debt they could not settle, he offered that woman his support and paid her debt himself. The saint then explained to him the reason for his question and told him about the vision that he had had. Touched by what he heard, the singer converted and became a monk.

But the biggest sinner encountered by Paphnutius was a woman of ill repute named Thaïs, who caused many men to fall into sin. To help her escape that way of life, the saint disguised himself as a man of the world, and once he was alone with her, he endeavored to convert her. He told her: "Can you show me a place where you will not be seen by anyone?" This made her conscious of the fact that God is everywhere. Consequently, nothing can be hidden from His eyes. The saint continued: "How, then, can we do evil in the presence of God?" The courtesan was shaken by these words.

She came to her senses and, by the help of grace, shed tears at the saint's feet, promising him that she would change her life and do penance. For her these were not empty promises! She immediately went to a monastery that Paphnutius pointed out to her and led a holy life for the rest of her days. She wept for her sins for three years in a sealed room, and soon afterward returned her soul to God. Paphnutius lived for another few years; he liked to recount these incidents to his monks to encourage them to avoid passing rash judgments on their neighbor.

Prayer

Teach me, O Lord, not to judge our neighbor for any fault that I may see him commit; and if I were to see him sin, give me the grace to excuse his intention, which is hidden and cannot be seen. But if I saw that the intention had been plainly evil, give me the grace to excuse my neighbor, because of the temptation from which no mortal man has been liberated.

—Fr. Gabriel, *ID*, vol. V, p. 28

Thoughts

- "Whither shall I go from Thy spirit [O Lord]? ... But darkness shall not be dark to Thee, and night shall be light as the day: the darkness thereof, and the light are alike to Thee."

    —Psalm 138:7, 12

- "Take care not to judge the actions of others. In judging others, a man wears himself out in vain; most often he is mistaken, and commits many errors; but by examining himself and personally judging himself, he always works fruitfully."

    —*The Imitation of Christ*, Book I, chap. 14

Resolutions

1. Recite the First Sorrowful Mystery for the conversion of a sinner.
2. Lift up your heart to God every hour of the day.
3. Avoid rash judgments, jumping to conclusions, and improper generalizations.

St. Winwaloe (Guénolé)

March 3

GOD SPEAKS TO US

Blessed are the meek: for they shall possess the land.
—Matthew 5:4

MEDITATION

The parents of St. Winwaloe (*ca.* 460-529) belonged to noble families in Wales. They had emigrated to Armorica shortly before his birth. During a violent storm, Fracan, Winwaloe's father, feared for his life. In the grip of fright, he offered his son to God. One week later, he and his wife brought him to Budoc, a holy man who lived in a monastery near the Isle of Bréhat (Côtes-d'Armor). Under the monk's direction, Winwaloe made rapid progress in virtue and received from God the gift of miracles. With a simple sign of the cross, he cured a child with an injured leg. He restored sight to his sister Clervia after a goose plucked out one of her eyes.

At the age of 21, after hearing about St. Patrick, the Apostle of Ireland, who had died 20 years earlier, Winwaloe had the desire to go and venerate his relics, but the saint appeared to Winwaloe, saying that he should remain on the continent and found a monastery there. Budoc was truly disappointed to lose such a perfect disciple. Nevertheless, he did not want to oppose the signs of Providence. So he let him leave, along with 11 of his monks, to found an abbey in Landévennec (Finistère). The region then was uninhabited and covered with woods, which required enormous labor in clearing the land so as to start farming and build various buildings: the church, the cloister, the refectory, the dormitory, the guest house, the farm, and its different workshops. Winwaloe's virtue and his miracles increased his reputation, to the point where King Gradlon came to offer him presents. Winwaloe refused the royal gifts. Nonetheless, he asked the king to protect his community from thieves. Full of missionary zeal, he brought a great number of barbarians to embrace the Christian religion.

Winwaloe was warned by God of his imminent death.

He then called his monks together, gave them a successor to replace him as the head of the monastery, and peacefully told them: "Prepare yourselves, because this very day, after I have sung the Mass, the Good Lord will call me back to Himself." And so it happened.

Attribute and Invocation

St. Winwaloe is depicted with a goose. He is invoked by the wives of sailors for the safety of their husbands who are at sea.

Prayer

O Jesus, meek and humble of heart, make my heart like unto Thine.

—Aspiration to the Sacred Heart

Or

[Lord Jesus,] teach me to respond humbly, gently, and with unfailing kindness to those who despise me or murmur against me.

—Fr. Gabriel, *ID*, vol. V, p. 55

Thoughts

- "Though he treated himself with great austerity, Winwaloe was not at all severe with others; he was easy-going and even-tempered. His face was marked by gentleness."

  —Liturgy, *Propre de Quimper*, 1851

- "Be like the bees: they bring nothing but honey to their hives. May your house be full of gentleness, peace, harmony, humility, and fervor."

  —Padre Pio, *PPJ*, September 8

Resolutions

1 Recite several times a day the aspiration cited above: *Jesus, meek and humble of heart....*

2 Take in the right way the remarks that people make to you.

3 Show gentleness to someone who is difficult to deal with while calling on his guardian angel.

St. Casimir

March 4

GOD SPEAKS TO US

Whosoever shall seek to save his life shall lose it, and whosoever shall lose it shall preserve it.

—St. Luke 17:33

MEDITATION

Some people claim that they are incapable of attaining holiness because of their social position. The obligations that they have in the world, they say, prevent them from sanctifying themselves. Yet we find saints in all strata of society. While some were slaves, others were sovereigns. It is true that the more you live in ease, the more difficult it is to remain sober and virtuous. Nevertheless, we have very fine, admirable examples, such as St. Casimir (1458-1484), a prince of royal blood. Son of the King of Poland, he was his father's associate in governing his country.

In order to attain perfection, he wondrously utilized the classic means that Holy Mother Church gives us: devotion to Our Lord's Passion and to Our Lady. He did not limit his acts of piety to a few routine prayers. He sought truly to live in the presence of God, spending long hours in prayer, especially during the night. When he attended the Holy Sacrifice of the Mass, his mind was so to speak transfigured at the moment of the consecration, so moved was he to see with the eyes of faith the Divine Victim come down upon the altar. He took very special care to preserve the virtue of purity. Thus, during the illness that led to his death, he refused the remedy that the physicians proposed to him, because the treatment could not be taken without committing a sin. In this way he manifested the degree of his attachment to God. He drew his strength from the practice of penitential exercises. Not only did he sleep beside his bed, but he used the discipline and wore a hair shirt in order to subdue the old man. Having pleased God, he was called back to Him at the age of 25. "Rest now in the bosom of eternal happiness, O Casimir, whom the grandeur of earthly things and all the pleasures of the courts could not distract from the great objective that had delighted your heart. Your life was short in duration, but fruitful in merits. Detach us from sin, which is man's greatest trouble because at the same time it greatly troubles God."[35]

Attributes, invocation, and patronage

St. Casimir is depicted with a crown and a scepter at his feet, holding a lily in his hand. He is invoked to overcome temptations against chastity. He is the patron saint of Poland and of Lithuania.

Prayer

O God, Thou didst strengthen St. Casimir with the virtue of constancy in the midst of royal delights and the snares of the world; we beseech Thee, grant by his intercession, that Thy faithful people may despise the things of the world and ever aspire to those of heaven. (Collect)

Thoughts

- "Every day, O my soul, pay your homage to Mary, solemnly celebrate her feasts, and proclaim her praises."
  —Exhortation read by St. Casimir

- "Honor the [Blessed Virgin], so that she may deliver you from the weight of your sins; call on her, so as not to be carried off by the torrent of the passions."
  —Exhortation read by St. Casimir

Resolutions

1. Meditate for 10 minutes on two Stations of the Cross.
2. Start preparing now for next Sunday's Mass by reading the proper prayers, and make an effort to arrive in plenty of time.
3. Recite three Hail Mary's in the evening to ask Our Lady for the grace of purity of body and heart.

---

[35] Dom Guéranger, *Année Liturgique*, septembre, p. 378.

St. John Joseph of the Cross

March 5

GOD SPEAKS TO US

We are fools for Christ's sake, but you are wise in Christ.
—I Corinthians 4:10

MEDITATION

Life nowadays is so comfortable that we rarely suffer from heat or cold, from hunger or thirst. Air conditioning in the summer, central heating in the winter, all the electric devices and modern means of transportation greatly facilitate our life. There is, however, a down side to this. Too often we are wimps and consequently vulnerable when confronting temptation. At the least trial, we tend to become discouraged, depressed, or turned in on ourselves. And so, in order to be strengthened interiorly, we must not forget to practice penance.

Reading the lives of the saints can serve this purpose very cuttingly. It shows us what people just like us have been capable of doing. John Joseph (Gian Giuseppe) of the Cross (1654-1734) from the Kingdom of Naples (Italy) led a heroic life in this respect. From the age of 16, he embraced the very austere life of the Discalced Monks of St. Peter of Alcantara. To the extremely rigorous Rule he added personal penances. For instance, he fastened to his shoulders a cross studded with sharp points, which caused him to have an incurable wound. He put another smaller one on his chest. For 30 years, he abstained from all drink and slept very little. Let us in turn likewise perform acts of mortification so as to subject our body totally to our mind, and our mind to God!

The holy monk's penances were marks of his love for Our Lord, who suffered so much to ransom us from our sins. Being a friend of God, he received from Him the gift of miracles. His biography relates incidents worthy of the Desert Fathers. One day, in the middle of February, the wife of a merchant in Naples fell seriously ill. She suffered a lot and, at the same time, she had a craving for peaches. Her husband, quite upset, told the saint about his wife's illness and about her craving for peaches. Father John Joseph reassured him, then asked Brother Pascal to plant some branches from the chestnut tree in a flowerpot. And the next day, miraculously, peaches adorned each one of the chestnut branches. Even the smallest desires of the merchant's wife were satisfied, and she very quickly was restored to full health. Despite all his austerities, St. John Joseph lived to the age of 80.

Prayer

O God, who didst raise thy Confessor, Blessed John Joseph, to heavenly glory by the austere paths of poverty, humility, and patience, grant, we beseech Thee, that by mortifying our flesh, we might imitate his example, and may merit the enjoyment of eternal happiness. (Collect)

Thoughts

- "He who always walks in the presence of God will never commit sins, but he will preserve his innocence and will become a great saint."
  —St. John Joseph of the Cross, *Pa S*, vol. III, p. 61

- "If neither heaven nor hell existed, I would nevertheless want to love God always. Let us love Our Lord really and in truth, because love for God is a genuine treasure."
  —St. John Joseph of the Cross, *Pa S*, vol. III, p. 63

Resolutions

1 Recite an Act of Hope with the firm intention that your requests will be granted. (See Appendix.)

2 Make an act of mortification during your next meal.

3 Turn off the screens so as to give priority to the interior life.

Saints Perpetua and Felicity

March 6

GOD SPEAKS TO US

Whosoever are led by the Spirit of God, they are the sons of God.

—Romans 8:14

MEDITATION

Sacred Scripture declares that "the life of man upon earth is a warfare" (Job 7:1). To see it through, man must demonstrate fortitude. But in some grave dangers. For the approach of martyrdom, mere virtue is not enough. It is necessary for God Himself to support a human being in order to enable him to triumph over them. By means of the gifts of the Holy Ghost, He strengthens the believer's soul and comes to the aid of his imperfection so as to guide him and make him capable of performing acts that surpass his natural abilities. Let us admire this action of the Holy Ghost in the souls of the two African women: Perpetual and Felicity (†203). Both of them, arrested in Carthage (Tunisia) with other Christians during the persecution of Septimus Severus, were condemned to be thrown to the wild animals. The first woman, around 22 years old, from a distinguished family, was married to a man of her rank. She had a baby who was not yet weaned. The second woman was a slave.

Perpetua's father was inconsolable when he learned that his daughter was condemned to death. He tried everything to make her apostatize, but it was wasted effort. His daughter remained unshakably devoted to Jesus Christ.

As for Felicity, she was about to give birth to a child. As the day of the execution approached, she was desolate at the thought that her pregnancy would postpone her agony, because the law forbade the execution of a pregnant woman. The other martyrs, too, were distressed about leaving her behind. Three days before the date appointed for the combat, they all started praying to obtain her prompt delivery. No sooner had they finished than she was seized by labor pains. As she was groaning, one of the jailers said to her: "If you cannot endure these sufferings now, what will you do when you are torn apart by the beasts? It would have been better if you had sacrificed to the gods." Felicity then gave this fine answer: "Today it is I who suffer, but then there will be Someone else in me who will suffer for me, because I will suffer for Him."[36] After giving birth to her child, she was beaten with rods along with Perpetua, then they were attacked by a mad cow, and finally they perished by the sword, having been made worthy of a "perpetual felicity" (*i.e.* eternal happiness).

O holy martyrs, assist us in our combat!

Prayer

Grant us, we beseech Thee, O Lord our God, to venerate with unceasing devotion the triumphs of Thy holy Martyrs, Perpetua and Felicity, so that, though we are not worthy to celebrate them, we may at least present to them our humble service. (Collect)

Thoughts

- "Our enemy conspires against us; towards the weak he makes himself strong, but he becomes a coward in the presence of those who confront him, weapon in hand."
  —Padre Pio, *PPJ*, April 23

- "Whoever relies on the Lord alone will always be light-hearted and triumphant."
  —Fr. Calmel, *365 J*, September 9

Resolutions

1 Recite the Fifth Sorrowful Mystery for the Christians who are being martyred today in Muslim countries.

2 Recite a *Memorare* for women who are seeking abortion. (See Appendix.)

3 Get down to work right away and finish what you start in order to grow stronger in the virtue of fortitude.

---

[36] Adapted from Père Froget, *De l'habitation du Saint-Esprit dans les âmes justes* (Tours: Lethielleux, 1938), 399-400.

St. Thomas Aquinas

March 7

GOD SPEAKS TO US

Blessed are the clean of heart, for they shall see God.
—St. Matthew 5:8

MEDITATION

Jesus said to His disciples: "Going, therefore, teach ye all nations" (Mt. 28:19). The Doctors of the Church would live up to His expectation by personally combining knowledge with eloquence, eloquence with piety, piety with sanctity. Among them, one man is distinguished by being loftier and more penetrating than the others: Thomas Aquinas (1225-1274). History has given him the nickname "Angelic Doctor." He owes his doctrine particularly to the virtue of purity, which he practiced to a heroic degree. When he was very little, his nurse took away the parchment that he held between his fingers, and he started to cry. When she unrolled it, she read on it these two words: *Ave Maria*. Thomas' Marian piety came before his attraction to learning. He would soon add to it an overflowing love for Jesus in the Sacred Host. At the age of five he was entrusted to the monks on Monte Cassino (Italy). These great educators would never again have such an attentive and brilliant pupil as he! Thomas continued his studies in Naples. To avoid going astray in that licentious city, he treasured his love for the Blessed Virgin and his zeal for work. He understood and remembered everything. He loved to follow the Divine Office in the church of the Dominicans. In front of the tabernacle, he deepened his knowledge of God. Soon he received the habit of St. Dominic there.

When she heard the news, his distraught mother came to take him back home, but he fled to Rome. She sought in vain by every means to divert him from his mission. One day, a courtesan came to tempt him at the castle in Rocca-Secca where his mother had confined him, but he went after her with a burning brand, then drew a cross with coal on the wall of his prison.

Because he had dominated his passions, St. Thomas received the grace of a penetrating understanding of truth. In his major work, the *Summa theologiae*, he studies God first, then man, his faculties, and the means by which he can return to God. Man is sanctified by the practice of the virtues, and the exercise of them is greatly facilitated by love for Jesus, the source and author of the Sacraments. According to Pope John XXII, St. Thomas spread more light in the Church than all the other Doctors combined. And so the crucifix in Naples that spoke to him in the Church of St. Dominic, gave this unique and glorious testimony which consecrates his teaching: "Thomas, you have written well about Me."

Attributes, Invocation, and Patronage

The attributes of St. Thomas are a book and a brilliant star on his chest. He is invoked against lust. He is the patron saint of Catholic teaching.

Prayer

O God, Thou givest glory to Thy Church by the wonderful learning of Blessed Thomas, Thy Confessor, and Thou makest it fruitful by his holy deeds; grant, we beseech Thee, that we may understand what he taught and follow his example in what he did. (Collect)

Thoughts

- "The more our soul distances itself from the love of earthly things, the more it is confirmed in the divine love."

　　　　　　　　　　　—St. Thomas Aquinas, *PPJ*, July 27

- "As you remember the lives and the actions of the saints, walk in their footsteps as much as you can, and humble yourselves if you cannot attain to their perfection."
　　　　　　　　　　—St. Thomas Aquinas, *Opusculum* 68

Resolutions

1. Recite the Fourth Joyful Mystery, asking for the virtue of purity and the grace to flee from dangerous occasions of sin.
2. Perform in an orderly way the duties of your state in life.
3. Read a chapter from a catechism or a book on doctrine.

St. John of God

March 8

GOD SPEAKS TO US

Better is one day in Thy courts, [O God,] above thousands [elsewhere].

—Ps. 83:11

MEDITATION

John of God (1495-1550) was born in Portugal. He had a turbulent childhood. He ran away at the age of eight and found himself the servant of a shepherd in Spain. He tended the sheep so well that his master offered him his daughter in marriage. He was 22 years old then. John refused and left that home to join the army. He went as far as Hungary, where he fought against the Turks. During that time he became spiritually lukewarm, but God brought him back to Him through various trials: a fall from a horse that could have been fatal for him, and the disappearance of the booty that he was in charge of. Upon returning to Spain, he went back to work as the shepherd's servant. Soon, however, shocked to see that the animals that his master tended were treated better than the beggars who knocked at his door, he had for the first time the idea of abandoning the care of animals to serve the poor. After another enlistment in the army and being discharged again, he hit on the idea of becoming a seller of pious images and books and other religious objects.

At the age of around 40, he made a general confession, so as to obtain guidance concerning his future. Shortly afterward, he heard a sermon given by St. John of Avila which impressed him so much that he profoundly regretted his sins and started to shout in the street: "Mercy, Lord, mercy!" He showed other signs of extravagance, to the point where he was confined to an asylum for several months. John of Avila went to visit him and told him that he had better things to do than to be singled out by his strange behavior. Indeed, few saints displayed their disdain for themselves to the same degree as he did. But from now on he would shine above all

St. John of God

by his charity: he founded a new Order that took the name of Brothers Hospitallers. Seeing that almsgiving is a work of mercy sure to touch God's heart, he went through the city of Grenada crying: "My brothers, for the love of God, do yourselves some good." One day, one of his hospices caught fire: John himself went in to look for the sick, carrying them in his arms so as to bring them out of danger. And God allowed him to pass through the flames without suffering any harm.

He died in prayer, clasping his crucifix to his heart.

Attributes and patronage

St. John of God is depicted with a crown of thorns and a cord around his neck, on which are hung two receptacles (for the alms). He is the patron saint of nurses, the dying, and booksellers.

Prayer

O God, Thou didst cause Blessed John, burning with love for Thee, to pass unharmed through flames, and through him Thou didst enrich Thy Church with a new offspring; grant, through his interceding merits, that our sinfulness may be healed in the fire of Thy love, and that we may receive healing remedies to life everlasting. (Collect)

Thoughts

- "Humility makes a person vanish, so that only God appears, to whom the glory should be given."
  —St. Vincent de Paul, *PPJ*, May 28

- "If the love of God is the fire, zeal is its flame; if the love of God is a sun, zeal is a ray from it."
  —St. Vincent de Paul, *PPJ*, July 17

Resolutions

1. Recite a decade of the Rosary for the insane and their families.
2. Visit someone who is sick.
3. Separate yourself from something useless out of a spirit of detachment.

St. Frances of Rome

March 9

God speaks to us

No evil shall come to thee, nor shall the scourge come near thy dwelling. For He hath given His angels charge over thee, to keep thee in all thy ways.

—Psalm 90:10-11

Meditation

Frances (1384-1440), a native of Rome, was married at the age of 12 and remained faithful to her husband for 40 years; she was a model wife and mother. She ended her days by joining the Oblate Benedictine Sisters of Mary, which she had founded. She was much loved, not only by her husband and their children, but also by the great dignitaries with whom she socialized and by the poor whom she served. To the innocence of her life she added the harshest penance by fasting, keeping vigil, wearing a hair shirt and an iron belt. By her austerities she reminds us that although God is infinitely merciful, He is also infinitely just. While generously pardoning a repentant soul, He expects her to make reparation for her disorders by acts of mortification and charity.

The devil, unable to bear the sight of such a holy soul, tormented her in various ways, but she always succeeded in frustrating his snares, thanks in particular to her guardian angel, with whom she was quite close. One night, while she was praying, the devil seized her by the hair, carried her onto the terrace of the house, and dangled her in the air above the street. God then intervened to bring her back into her room.

Another angel, who ranked higher than her guardian angel, had been granted to the saint to help her make spiritual progress and to punish her if ever she was unfaithful. At the slightest fault, he would strike her, even in public. One day, she was with persons who were having a thoughtless conversation. She felt that she should intervene to bring them into line, but at that moment she did not dare to do so, out of weakness. Immediately she received a resounding slap that everyone heard.

"O Frances! Have pity on us who are still so far from the right path on which you walked. Help us to become Christians; subdue in us the love for the world and its vanities, bend us down under the weight of penance, call us back to humility, strengthen us in temptations."[37]

ATTRIBUTES, INVOCATION, AND PATRONAGE

St. Frances is depicted as a religious with an angel beside her or carrying a bundle of sticks on her back. She is invoked against intrusions of a mother-in-law into a household. She is the patron saint of the city of Rome and of automobile drivers.

PRAYER

O God, among other gifts of Thy grace, Thou didst honor Blessed Frances, Thy handmaid, with the familiar presence of an angel; grant, we beseech Thee, that through her intercession, we may be worthy to attain the fellowship of angels. (Collect)

THOUGHTS

- "Oh, if we were like the guardian angels! They continually see God and at the same time always care for us. This is because God is their absolute center."
  —St. Peter Julian Eymard, *PPJ*, October 2
- "The good angel keeps watch to put a good thought into a person's mind as soon as he wakes up."
  —St. Vincent de Paul, *PPJ*, October 2

RESOLUTIONS

1. Call on your guardian angel several times a day, especially when traveling and at the start of an activity.
2. Make a sacrifice in the spirit of reparation for your sins.
3. Bring your neighbor into line when he offends God by his thoughtless conversations, or show your disapproval.

---

[37] Dom Guéranger, *AL,* septembre, p. 419.

The Forty Martyrs of Sebaste

March 10

GOD SPEAKS TO US

Blessed shall you be when men shall hate you .... Be glad in that day and rejoice: for behold, your reward is great in heaven.
—Gospel: St. Luke 6:22-23

MEDITATION

To encourage us to embrace valiantly the law of Lenten penance, the Church presents us with more heroes of the faith: the 40 martyrs of Sebaste (†320) in Armenia (today Sivas in Turkey). They were part of the *Fulminans* Legion under the Emperor Licinius. They were brought before the judge for having refused to sacrifice to the idols. After a stay in prison, their faces were scraped with stones, then they were exposed naked for a whole night in the dead of winter on a frozen pond. The mere thought of that torture horrifies us!

Nevertheless, supported by divine strength, the valiant legionaries offered to God this prayer: "Lord, 40 of us have been arrested to undergo martyrdom. You sanctified this number 40 by Your stay in the desert before Your public life, and before that Moses and Elias too had fasted for the same length of time; therefore assure that none of us abandons the fight during the sufferings that they are inflicting on us."

While the guards were resting, the doorkeeper saw a great light surround the soldiers and angels descending from heaven with 39 crowns. He wondered: "Where is the crown of the fortieth legionary?" At that moment, he saw one of the 40 give up because of the harsh cold and go to a bath of warm water, the sign of his apostasy.

The doorkeeper, filled with admiration for the Christians' heroic attitude, and trusting in the divine mercy after hearing the soldiers' prayer, awakened the guards and told them that he was a Christian. Thus he joined the martyrs.

The Forty Martyrs of Sebaste

The guards then hurried to break the legs of the martyrs, and they all died during that torture except for the youngest. His heroic mother encouraged him not to weaken in his faith so close to the goal. In fact, he died shortly afterward. Thus the number of martyrs was brought to 40 according to the soldiers' prayer. Their bodies were consumed by the flames.

O holy martyrs of Sebaste, help us to strip ourselves of the old man during Lent. We will manage to conquer the enemies of our souls by our faith in the word of God, hope in His help, humility, and prudence. O holy martyrs, you are our comrades in arms; hasten to come help us, so that we in turn might merit the crown of glory in a blessed eternity.

Prayer

Grant, we beseech Thee, almighty God, that we who acknowledge the courage of Thy glorious Martyrs in confessing Thy name, may experience their loving intercession for us with Thee. (Collect)

Thoughts

- "The Holy Ghost is a force.... He is the one who supported the martyrs. Without the Holy Ghost, the martyrs would have fallen like the leaves of the trees."
—The Curé of Ars, St. John Vianney, *PPJ2*, October 26

- "Only by looking beyond this world, where everything passes away and dies, can we find true joy in the hope for another life, of which this one is only the prelude."
—Charles de Foucauld, *PPJ*, November 4

Resolutions

1 Practice the devotion of the Five First Saturdays of the month in order to assure your final perseverance.

2 Do not complain about the cold or bad weather.

3 Make a sacrifice in union with present-day martyrs.

St. Pol of Léon

March 11 (celebrated on the 12th)

GOD SPEAKS TO US

The Lord made with him a covenant of peace, to be the prince of the sanctuary and of His people, that the dignity of the priesthood should be to him and to his seed for ever.
—Introit: Ecclesiasticus 45:30

MEDITATION

Finistère (Brittany) owes its Christianization in large part to St. Corentin and to St. Pol of Léon; both of them lived in the sixth century.

Pol of Léon (492-572), with the surname Aurelian, was born in Great Britain. His father, chief of the clan of South Wales, wanted to train him to bear arms, but observing his attraction to the religious life, had him enter a monastery headed by a disciple of St. Germanus of Auxerre.

At the age of 16, Pol, with the approval of his spiritual director, withdrew for several years as a hermit, until the time when he received Holy Orders at around the age of 22. Then he became abbot of a monastery of about 12 monks. He wore a simple habit and had a very strict diet, being content with bread and water during the week and simply adding some vegetables and fish on Sundays.

Not wishing to be raised to the episcopal dignity, he boarded a boat with his monks and, guided by an angel, traveled to the Island of Ushant (Ouessant). After staying there for several months, he returned to the region of Léon on the continent.

Count Withur granted to him the Island of Batz and a ruined fortress on the continent. Pol founded his monastery on the island and a daughter house in the fortress as the home base for evangelizing the region. He restored sight to three blind men, speech to two mutes, made a fountain spring up in an arid place, and liberated the island from a dragon.

Since he could not manage to make Pol agree to be consecrated a bishop, the count soon commissioned him to travel to

Paris to transmit a message to King Childebert I. Pol did not know the contents of it. In it the lord begged the king to give Pol the dignity of Bishop of Léon. Childebert convinced Pol to accept it and asked three bishops to consecrate him, then sent him back to Armorica. St. Pol established his episcopal see in the town which today bears his name.

Faithful to the duties of his office, he converted many pagans, destroyed the shrines dedicated to the false gods, and founded churches and monasteries.

However, still having the same attraction to the solitary life, at the end of his life, after handing on his episcopacy to one of his disciples, he withdrew to his beloved monastery on the Island of Batz, where he gave up his beautiful soul to God at a very advanced age.

Attributes

St. Pol is depicted as a bishop, with a dragon at his feet.

Prayer

O God, who by the apostolic ministry of Thy Bishop, St. Pol, didst design to enrich an unbelieving people with the light of faith, grant us by Thy favor and his intercession to obtain by upright conduct the glory promised to Thy faithful ones. (Collect)

Thoughts

- "Let us be silent so as to hear the One who has so much to say to us."
  —Elizabeth of the Trinity, *PPJ*, July 20

- "We must begin by establishing the kingdom of God in ourselves, and then in others."
  —St. Vincent de Paul, *PPJ*, August 31

Resolutions

1 Recite the Third Glorious Mystery for the conversion of a close friend.

2 Make silent time a priority so as to live closer to God.

3 Tell the story of a saint from your region to your children or friends for their edification.

St. Gregory the Great

March 12

GOD SPEAKS TO US

If you love Me, Simon Peter, feed My lambs.
—Introit: St. John 21:15-17

MEDITATION

Son of Senator Gordianus and St. Sylvia, Gregory the Great (540-604) held various honorable offices in the world. He was senator, then prefect of the city of Rome, dignities which he finally renounced in order to embrace the utmost poverty. He kept only a silver bowl in which his mother sent him beans for his food. But one day he ended up parting with it, too, so as to give it to a poor merchant who had lost all his belongings as a result of a shipwreck.

He received the Benedictine habit in St. Andrew Monastery in Rome. He devoted himself to reading the Holy Books. Without neglecting the literal sense of Sacred Scripture, he paid special attention to its symbolic meaning. He gave to each event in the Bible an interpretation that is perfectly adapted to our human nature and applied it to the world in which he lived. His purpose was to lead human beings to love God with their whole heart and to love their neighbor for the love of God. Furthermore, he subdued his flesh so much that it affected his health for the rest of his life.

He was ordained deacon and, shortly afterward, was appointed nuncio to Constantinople. When Pope Gelasius died, he was called to succeed him. Upon his elevation to the office of Supreme Pontiff he received letters of congratulations, and he responded with tears and groans. He bitterly missed the time when he could dedicate himself to contemplating God. He had on his shoulders the weight of all the local churches. Every nation had its particular trial to confront: "In Africa, Donatism; in Spain, Arianism; in England, idolatry; in Gaul, Frédégonde and Brunehaut; in Italy, the Lombards; in the East, the arrogance of the patriarchs of Constantinople. St. Gregory's solicitude extended everywhere."[38] Often confined to bed, he nevertheless kept his soul serene so as to fulfill all his obligations. Far from thinking that he was superior to others because of the dignity of his office, he still had a humble opinion of himself. He signed his letters with the formula that has become famous: "Servant of the servants of God." He is one of the four great Doctors of the Latin Church.

ATTRIBUTES, INVOCATION, AND PATRONAGE

St. Gregory is depicted as Pope with a dove, the symbol of the Holy Ghost. He is invoked to relieve the souls in purgatory. He is the patron saint of cantors.

PRAYER

O God, Thou hast given to the soul of Thy servant Gregory the rewards of everlasting bliss; grant that we, who are oppressed by the weight of our sins, may be relieved by his intercession with Thee. (Collect)

THOUGHTS

- "May each one, in the measure of his strength, subdue his flesh and diminish its desires, may he put to death its shameful covetousness so as to become, as St. Paul says, a living sacrifice" (Rom. 12:1).
  —St. Gregory the Great, *PPJ*, February 22

- "What is more exalted than humility? By demeaning itself very low, it is united to its Creator, who dwells above the highest things."
  —St. Gregory the Great, *PPJ*, August 27

RESOLUTIONS

1. Recite the Third Glorious Mystery for the Pope's intentions.

2. In order to fulfill all your obligations faithfully, begin with what you like the least.

3. Avoid efforts to impress others.

---

[38] Ernest Hello, *Physionomies de saints*, p. 79.

St. Euphrasia

March 13

GOD SPEAKS TO US

Hear, O daughter, and see; turn your ear; for the King shall desire your beauty.

—Tract: Psalm 44:11-12

MEDITATION

Euphrasia (382-412) was a relative of the Emperor Theodosius. Her father held the office of Governor of Lycia, but died shortly after her birth. Her mother then retired with her to the Thebaid (Egypt) and settled near a monastery with 139 nuns. Very pious, she often traveled to the convent with her daughter, who was then seven years old.

One day the mother superior asked the child this question: "Whom do you love better, the sisters or the Senator's son who was promised to you in marriage?" And she answered, "I do not know him, but I know you and I love you." The superior told her: "We, too; we love you and Jesus Christ, our Lord." The child replied: "And I love you, and Jesus Christ your Lord." "If you love us," the abbess said, laughing, "stay and live with us." Taking her literally, the child answered her very seriously, "I would like that very much, but only if my mother approves." The mother heard with emotion this delightful conversation, which at the same time was agonizing for her maternal heart. The abbess continued, explaining to little Euphrasia that in order to become a nun, it is necessary to consecrate oneself to Jesus. The girl asked her, "Where is He?" The superior showed her a crucifix, which the child immediately kissed, and she added that in order to live with the nuns, she would have to learn the psalms and fast every day. Plainly, these rules did not appear to trouble the child in the least. So it was that little Euphrasia became a nun. Her mother died shortly afterward. The emperor then informed her that it was time for her to marry the one to whom she had been promised. She answered him that she had chosen to take Jesus Christ as her spouse, and she asked him to dispose of her property for the benefit of the poor and to free her slaves, which he did.

At the age of 12, Euphrasia was content with one meal per day. Later on she could on occasion go for a whole week without eating. In her community, she edified the nuns by her virtues. She joyfully performed the most modest tasks, such as sweeping the convent, cutting wood, drawing water from the well for the needs of the house. The Superior put her to the test in various ways to extinguish whatever self-love she had left. Nevertheless, her virtue aroused the jealousy of the nuns, who treated her as a hypocrite, but these calumnies disturbed neither her patience nor her serenity. At the age of 30, she fell seriously ill and gave her beautiful soul back to God.

Prayer

Hear our prayer, O God our Savior; grant that, in our joy over celebrating the virgin, Blessed Euphrasia, we might also be animated by feelings of fervent piety. (Collect)

Thoughts

- "Jesus came to meet me. He took me in His arms to carry me like a little child."
  —Elizabeth of the Trinity, *PPJ*, January 12

- "We must thank Him all the time, whatever happens, because the Good Lord is Love and can do nothing but Love."
  —Elizabeth of the Trinity, *PPJ*, January 22

Resolutions

1. Recite the Fifth Sorrowful Mystery to ask God to raise up vocations of contemplative nuns.
2. Meditate for 15 minutes on the Passion of Christ or three stations of the Way of the Cross.
3. Serenely accept disagreeable remarks without trying to justify yourself.

St. Matilda

March 14

GOD SPEAKS TO US

Put ye on therefore, as the elect of God, heartfelt mercy.
—Epistle of St. Paul to the Colossians 3:12

MEDITATION

Matilda (875-968) was raised by her grandmother, Abbess of the Benedictines in Erfurt, in Thuringia (Germany). Nature had showered its gifts on her: she was very beautiful physically, her character was very amiable, active, pure, and generous. Amazed by so many good qualities, Otto of Saxony asked for her in marriage for his son, Henry the Bird-Catcher, the future Emperor of Germany. From her union with Henry I three sons and two daughters were born: Otto, who would succeed his father as Emperor; Henry, who would become Duke of Bavaria; Bruno, future Archbishop of Cologne; Gerberge, future wife of Louis IV, King of France; and Hedwig, who would marry Hugh the Great, father of Hugh Capet. When she had become Queen of Germany, far from letting herself be ensnared by worldliness and vanity, she humbled herself instead all the more before God. She customarily mortified herself and did penances, and she devoted all her free time to prayer and works of charity.

The most difficult trial that she endured was the death of her husband after 23 years of life spent together in the most perfect concord. She consoled herself with the thought that a day would come when she would meet him again in a blessed eternity. She exhorted her children to preserve their love for God and to remain united with one another. Unfortunately, not all of them followed her wise counsels. Indeed, her son Otto, once he had ascended the throne, proved to be an ungrateful son, and so did Henry, to whom nevertheless she had shown until then a preferential love. The two brothers blamed her for squandering the royal treasure. The Emperor went so far as to divest her of what she possessed, then he sent her into exile. Matilda did not rebel against this flagrant injustice and his deplorable attitude. She accepted this new trial in the spirit of faith. She took refuge in a convent in Westphalia. Finally, Otto, having been tested in various ways, returned to his senses with regard to his mother and made reparation for his unworthy conduct by asking her forgiveness and begging her to return to his palace. Henry, in turn, acknowledged the wrong that he had done.

From then on the Queen dedicated her time to good works. With Otto's approval, she had churches, hospitals, and other religious houses built. She arose at night so that in the morning, before the cock crowed, she had already recited the 150 psalms. At the end of her life, she retired to a convent and, sensing that her death was near, she made a confession, had a Mass celebrated, and received Holy Communion. As a sign of humility, she died lying on a hair shirt and asked for her face to be covered with ashes.

Prayer

Our Father, who art in heaven, ... forgive us our trespasses, as we forgive those who trespass against us.

—*Our Father*

Thoughts

- "Will someone who is convinced of his own frailty, weakness, and inconstancy have the audacity to condemn others?"

  —Fr. Gabriel, *ID*, vol. V, p. 197

- "As sinners, we have an infinite need of God's forgiveness. Let us forgive, and let us hope for everything from His mercy in time and in a blessed eternity."

  —Bourdaloue, *OEC*, vol. II, p. 408

Resolutions

1 Recite the First Joyful Mystery, asking the Blessed Virgin for the virtue of humility.

2 Put an end to a difference of opinion with a relative.

3 Examine the way in which you are raising your children.

St. Louise de Marillac

March 15

GOD SPEAKS TO US

Who shall find a valiant woman? Far and from the uttermost coasts is the price of her.

—Book of Proverbs 31:10

MEDITATION

Louise de Marillac (1591-1660) lost her mother shortly after her birth. Her father remarried. Louise was then placed under the tutelage of the Dominican Nuns of Poissy, then of a virtuous instructress. Having met holy religious women, she had the desire to enter the religious life. However, at around the age of 22, she married. In late 1613 she brought into the world a little son, Michael, and proved to be very attentive to him and affectionate. Nevertheless, after the death of her husband (†1625), she decided to dedicate herself to God, and for that purpose placed herself under the spiritual direction of St. Vincent de Paul.

He invited her to visit the Confraternities of Charity that he had founded in Paris, and to increase the number of them. From May 1626 until 1628, Louise led a religious life in the world, with a strict rule of life concerning piety and the care to be given to the poor and the sick. When her son entered the seminary of Saint-Nicolas-du-Chardonnet, this gave her more freedom to devote herself to manifold works: retreats, little schools, orphanages, hospitals. Thus she was at the origin of the Company of the Daughters of Charity (1634), whose mission is to relieve human misery in all its forms. However, she did not forget that one cannot give what one does not have. Therefore, she invited her daughters to perfect themselves "so as to keep doing more and better, to become better and holier, to do more good all around them." By the end of one year, with the support of the first Daughters of Charity, she had the consolation of being instrumental in 760 conversions. The years 1641 and following were the most prosperous. During that period, some of the Daughters of Charity were admitted to take annual vows under the authority of St. Vincent de Paul and St. Louise. Despite her failing health, the foundress dedicated herself totally to the care of the sick, to the works that she had founded, and to the formation of new recruits. She spent her final years in peace and calm, and when she died on March 15, 1660, St. Vincent de Paul was able to testify: "She was a strong woman, a saint."[39]

INVOCATION AND PATRONAGE

St. Louise de Marillac is invoked for the sick and for the neglected elderly. She is the patron saint of those who dedicate themselves to Christian social works.

PRAYER

O God, author and reward of charity, who didst cause a new religious family to be born in Thy Church and wast pleased to give it Blessed Louise as its mother, graciously grant that by performing the works of charity, we might merit to obtain the promised reward in heaven. (Collect)

THOUGHTS

- "You must treat the poor with great gentleness and respect, keeping in mind that they are supposed to open heaven for you."
 —St. Vincent de Paul, *PPJ*, October 10

- "We should take a look at Louise de Marillac.... After her example, make the resolution to work to become perfect and to detach yourself from anything in you that displeases God."
 —St. Vincent de Paul, *PPJ*, March 15

---

[39] *Conference given to the Daughters of Charity*, 1660, vol. X, pp. 709-736.

Resolutions

1. Recite the Second Joyful Mystery, asking God to raise up active women religious.
2. Come to the aid of a poor person or say three *Hail Mary*'s for his intention.
3. Do not criticize active or teaching nuns.

The Holy Canadian Martyrs

March 16

GOD SPEAKS TO US

I tell you, my friends, [said Jesus]: Do not be afraid of those who persecute you.

—Communion: paraphrase of Luke 12:4

MEDITATION

Two Jesuits had been sent to Nova Scotia as early as 1608, but not until 1632 was a mission center established in Quebec by the Jesuits. Paul Le Jeune, Superior of the Mission, was joined the following year by Jean de Brébeuf, Antoine Daniel, and Ennemond Massé.

The life of the Indians had its annoyances. The Indians suffered from the heat, the cold, the dogs, and the smoke. Men, women, and dogs slept together around the fire, and the smoke irritated them to the point where some of them lost their sight.

The first mission was inaugurated among the Hurons, comprising 20,000 inhabitants dispersed in 30 villages. The obstacles to the conversion of the Indians came above all from their way of life: their laws about marriage, the practice of torture, their cannibal feasts. Since the plague of 1638 coincided with the arrival of five missionaries, the Indians concluded that the Jesuits were "bearers of misfortune." The Iroquois tribe, which had been conquered by the French 30 years previously, was the enemy of the Hurons.

René Goupil (1606-1642) was killed with a tomahawk blow by an Iroquois for having dared to baptize a child. Isaac Jogues (1607-1646) was imprisoned, but he managed to escape after several weeks. After a stay in France, he returned to Canada in 1644. There he succumbed with Jean de La Lande (1606-1646) after being tortured. While still wearing his priestly vestments after celebrating Mass, Antoine Daniel (*ca.* 1600-1648), the curate of a Huron village of 2,000 inhabitants, approached the Iroquois who had come to destroy his village. They pierced him with arrows, then killed him with a gunshot.

The following year, Jean de Brébeuf (1593-1649) and Gabriel Lalemant (1610-1649) endured indescribable tortures: burning, mutilation, and being boiled in water. Finally, the former had his heart torn out while the latter had his skull crushed by hatchet blows. Charles Garnier (1606-1649) was killed while trying to give absolution to a dying Indian. Noël Chabanel (1613-1649) suffered the same fate, killed by a Huron apostate.

That was the end of the mission among the Hurons, whose conversion had been brought about very slowly.

Patronage

These holy martyrs are the patron saints of Canada.

Prayer

O God, who didst will that the word and the blood of Thy martyrs, Jean de Brébeuf, Isaac Jogues, and their companions, should sanctify the beginnings of the Church in North America, grant that, by their prayers, a harvest of Christians may arise everywhere more abundantly each day. (Collect)

Thoughts

- "True charity is to love one's friend in God and to love one's enemy for God."
  —St. Gregory the Great, *PPJ*, January 13

- "Battles bring us to the foot of the cross, and the cross brings us to the gate of heaven."
  — The Curé of Ars, St. John Vianney, *PPJ2*, November 12

Resolutions

1. Recite a decade of the Rosary for missionaries, that they might have the courage to preach the faith, at the risk of their life, if necessary.
2. Obey God in little things so as to have the grace to remain faithful to Him in important ones.
3. Make a sacrifice to obtain the conversion of an unbeliever.

St. Patrick

March 17

GOD SPEAKS TO US

Behold the great priest who, in his days, pleased God and was found just.

—Introit: Ecclesiasticus 44:16

MEDITATION

Patrick (389-461) was probably born in Wales. Around 404, when Irish pirates pillaged his family farm, he was sold to a master who put him to work tending his flocks. Somewhat negligent until then in his pious exercises, the rigor of exile led him to turn to God, as he writes in his *Confession*. He wanted to merit his freedom by leading an increasingly holy life. During those six years of captivity, he learned to speak Gaelic. He ended up escaping, and he arrived at a port that he did not know and found a place on a boat. When the ship docked, the pagans who were on board were famished. Patrick reassured them, started to pray, and his prayer was answered immediately. A herd of swine appeared, to the great joy of everyone, and thus they were able to get fresh supplies. When he returned to his country, he was exiled a second time for two months. When he returned home, his parents urged him not to leave again, but God made known to him by a revelation that He was calling him to evangelize Ireland.

In order to receive suitable doctrinal formation, he traveled to Gaul, as far as the islands of Lérins, then went on to Italy. Next, he stayed in Auxerre for more than 15 years (415-432). There, he received a solid formation from two great bishops, Amator (†418), then St. Germanus (†448). He sought a life of deeper union with God and combined it with the study of Sacred Scripture and dogmas. He received episcopal consecration from the hands of Germanus. He was then ready for his great mission of evangelizing Ireland.

With the soul of a conqueror, he got down to the work of converting the kings, or the tribal chiefs, for they alone could grant him plots of ground on which to build churches. He had a modicum of success. Sometimes he did not treat his adversaries gently. A crowd of wizards tried to prevent him from entering their region. Patrick cursed their chief, Rechrad, who fell down dead stiff at his feet. He baptized thousands of people, as he himself relates. Before admitting them to baptism, he asked the neophytes to acknowledge the dogma of the Trinity and that of the Eucharist. Being a man of faith, he expected everything from God and brought everything back to God. Acts of violence, threats, and captivity neither shook his faith nor diminished his courage. He drew his strength from prayer. He spent his final years in retreat before receiving the worthy reward from Our Lord, whom he loved and served so well.

Attributes and patronage

St. Patrick is depicted as a bishop with serpents at his feet or else with a three-leafed clover. He is the patron saint of Ireland.

Prayer

O God, Thou didst deign to send Blessed Patrick, Thy Confessor and Bishop, to preach Thy glory to the Gentiles; by his merits and intercession, grant that those things which Thou commandest us to do, we may be enabled to accomplish by Thy mercy. (Collect)

Thoughts

- "To be a missionary is to let one's heart overflow."
— The Curé of Ars, St. John Vianney, *PPJ2*, October 21

- I"t is necessary to work in this world, it is necessary to fight. We will have plenty of time to rest throughout eternity."
— The Curé of Ars, St. John Vianney, *PPJ2*, September 19

Resolutions

1 Recite a decade of the Rosary, asking for the conversion of a prisoner.

2 Recite the *Apostles' Creed* with attention and devotion.

3 Read the chapter from your catechism on the dogma of the Trinity or on the Holy Eucharist.

St. Cyril of Jerusalem
March 18

GOD SPEAKS TO US

Many will praise his understanding; his fame can never be effaced.

—Epistle: Ecclesiasticus 39:12

MEDITATION

Cyril (*ca.* 315-386) was born in Jerusalem. He lived during a troubled time because of the raging Arianism, a heresy that denied the divinity of Jesus Christ. He devoted himself with the utmost care to Sacred Scripture, so much so that all his speeches would be imbued with it. He received priestly ordination from the hands of St. Maximus in 345. He had the grace to prepare catechumens for Baptism. His *Catecheses* would make him famous. Several years later, he was consecrated a bishop and was assigned to the See of Jerusalem. This heavy responsibility was not exactly restful. Indeed, of his 37 years in the episcopate, he spent seventeen in exile. He met in particular with the fierce opposition of Acacius of Caesarea, an Arian bishop, and from the Arian Emperor Constantius. He was a contemporary of St. Athanasius and his defender against the heretics.

One day, an immense cross appeared in the sky, covering all Jerusalem from west to east. All the inhabitants of Jerusalem saw it, so that a large number of pagans converted. St. Cyril also witnessed the attempt by Julian the Apostate[40] to prove the Scriptures wrong by trying to rebuild the Temple of Jerusalem. In order to establish a basis for the new building, the workmen started destroying the old foundations; when they were preparing to make new ones, "horrible whirlwinds of flames shot out from the places adjacent to the foundations, burned the workmen, and made the place inaccessible to them… [so that] they were obliged to abandon the project."

---

[40] Ammianus Marcellinus (pagan author, friend of Julian the Apostate), *Res gestae*, XXIII, 1.

In 381, Cyril participated in the Second Ecumenical Council, the first in Constantinople. There, he recalled that the Father and the Son are of the same nature and that the Holy Ghost is God. He was a great devotee of the sign of the cross.

O St. Cyril, ardent defender of the Catholic faith, help me to be proud of my faith, to nourish it by an upright life, and to propagate it zealously.

Attributes

St. Cyril is depicted as a bishop with a purse, sign of his generosity to the poor.

Prayer

Grant us, we beseech Thee, O almighty God, by the intercession of the Blessed Bishop Cyril, so to know Thee, the only true God, and Jesus Christ, Whom Thou has sent, that we may deserve to be numbered forevermore with the sheep who hear His voice. (Collect)

Thoughts

- "Christ had His most-pure hands and His feet pierced by nails, and He suffered. And although I have not suffered or toiled, He gives salvation to me, communicating to me the fruit of His sufferings."
  — St. Cyril of Jerusalem, *Catecheses*, XX, 5

- "Christ once changed water into wine, which resembles blood, at Cana in Galilee, and should we not believe Him when He changes wine into His blood?"
  — St. Cyril of Jerusalem, *Catecheses*, XXII, 1-2

Resolutions

1 Recite the Fifth Sorrowful Mystery to thank Our Lord for having given His life for us.

2 Make a spiritual communion. (See Appendix.)

3 Be very attentive every time you make the sign of the cross.

St. Joseph (1)

March 19

GOD SPEAKS TO US

The angel of the Lord appeared to him in his sleep, saying: "Joseph, son of David, fear not to take unto thee Mary thy wife, for that which is conceived in her, is of the Holy Ghost."
—Matthew 1:20-21

MEDITATION

How should we understand these few words from the Gospel today? St. Joseph is the virginal spouse of Mary, the holiest of all women, the perfect model of all virtues. A just man of royal lineage, St. Joseph knew the Scriptures well; he could not have been unaware of this prophecy by Isaias: "Behold a virgin shall conceive and bear a son: and his name shall be called Emmanuel" (Is. 7:14). When he saw that Mary was expecting a child, St. Joseph understood that she was this Virgin who had been foretold. In his great humility he felt unworthy to remain close to the woman whom God had chosen to be the Mother of His Son. He therefore decided to put her away discreetly.[41] That was when the Lord communicated a secret to him in a dream: the great mystery of the Incarnation, with a view to the Redemption. Since His Son needed a foster father here on earth and the Mother of God needed a protector, Providence entrusted these two missions to him.

St. Joseph accepted them with an admirable faith, and he carried them out with courageous obedience. His whole life is summed up as a perfect submission to the divine plan, even though it included very mysterious and obscure situations. In our lives, too, there is always a bit of mystery. Indeed, as God repeated many times in the Sacred Scriptures, His ways are not our ways; His plans are not our plans.

---

[41] This is the opinion of St. Jerome, St. Bernard, and other Doctors of the Church, reported by Father Giry in his *Vie des Saints* [Life of the Saints] (Paris, 1865).

Good St. Joseph, help me always to say Yes to God and not to worry when, in my life, I find myself facing darkness, difficulties, and mystery.

On your feast day, I also want to ask you to watch over all the families on earth, and particularly mine. May you support all the fathers of the world in their role as spouses, heads of families, and educators.[42]

Patronage

St. Joseph is the patron saint of carpenters and of a happy death.

Prayer

All for Jesus, all for Mary, all in imitation of you, O patriarch Joseph! This will be my motto in life and in death. Amen.

— Prayer of Pius X to St. Joseph[43]

Thoughts

- "O Joseph, in your life everything happened as it does in ours. And how many trials, labors, and dangers! Oh, how astonished we would be if we know all that you suffered!"

    — Fr. Gabriel, *ID*, vol. II, p. 253

- "Let us ask Our Lord to give us the grace to say as He did: 'My food is to do the will of Him who sent me'" (Jn. 4:34).

    — St. Vincent de Paul, XII, p. 164

Resolutions

1 Imitate St. Joseph's promptness in obeying.

2 Choose the areas in which it is absolutely necessary to be a good example for children, and write them down in a notebook.

3 Pray to St. Joseph, Patron of the Universal Church, for the Church.

---

[42] To understand better the role of a father, refer to our book *La Famille catholique* (Clovis, 2011).

[43] *Prières et oeuvres pies* (Marietti, 1938), p. 333.

St. Joseph (2)
March 20

GOD SPEAKS TO US

And he came to dwell in a city called Nazareth.
—Matthew 2:23

MEDITATION

St. Joseph is the head of a family which is the sacred model of Catholic homes. And so today, let us contemplate him again, this time during his life in Nazareth.

St. Joseph teaches us how to sanctify our work. Indeed, in his everyday tasks, he does not lose the presence of God. Each of his strokes with the plane or the saw is an act of love. The spirit of prayer is the atmosphere that St. Joseph's soul breathes. He revels more each day in his union with God. Raised to this height, he can see the relative insignificance of the concrete realities of life here below. Of course, he loves Judea, the country of his fathers, Jerusalem the city of the Temple, Bethlehem the town of his ancestors; he loves his relatives, his neighbors, his friends, and much more his very gentle Spouse, and above all Jesus the Divine Child; but all these dear ties he loves only as much as the Good Lord permits. He is therefore ready to sacrifice them if the will of the Father demands it, because he analyzes all events of the present life with the eyes of faith.

Since he leads his whole family according to God's will, the result is great peace. Who could describe the intimate union, the grace, the holiness, the heavenly love that reigned in the home of Nazareth? Let us contemplate the Holy Family and strive to make ours similar to it. Let us defend in our homes the same piety, the same purity, the same charity. Our houses will then very quickly become vestibules of paradise.

Our enemies today are attacking the family. The family is strong because it is united. "And so," they say, "let us divide it by divorce." It is strong because it is pure; "Let us do all that we can to unleash passions everywhere." It is strong because of its charity; "Let us destroy charity by proclaiming the reign of selfishness." Let us be vigilant so as not to fall into these traps that are set for us.

St. Joseph also gives us a fine example by his methodical, regular, and constant work. He spares no effort and supports his family by the sweat of his brow. Here again, he teaches us that happiness here below does not reside in wealth, but in peace of mind, in union with God, and in labor that is sometimes hidden but always fruitful in God's sight.

Finally, as we recalled yesterday, God allowed the life of St. Joseph to be strewn with trials so that we might learn not to be discouraged by the difficulties of life.

Prayer

Help us, O Joseph, mirror of the most admirable fatherhood…, be with us in our joyful hours and in our sad hours, in our works and in our rest.

— Pius XII

Thoughts

- "Bear very patiently with the weaknesses of others, their bodily weaknesses and their character faults."
— St. Benedict, *PPJ*, February 19

- "Why support yourself? Because in doing this, we fulfill the law of Jesus Christ: 'Bear one another's burdens and so you shall fulfill the law of Christ'" (Gal. 6:2).
— St. Vincent de Paul, *PPJ*, April 18

Resolutions

1 Recite an act of charity. (See Appendix.)

2 Live a little more in the presence of God, imitating St. Joseph.

3 Discreetly perform some service at home that will give pleasure to all the members of the family.

Prayers

Spiritual Communion

Spiritual communion consists in an ardent desire to receive Jesus in the Host, and in an act of love such as one would make if one had received Him sacramentally.[44] The Council of Trent strongly praises spiritual communion and encourages the faithful to practice it.[45]

To make a good spiritual communion, St. Alphonsus Liguori recommends the following act:

> My Jesus, I believe that Thou art Present in the Blessed Sacrament. I Love Thee above all things, and I desire Thee in my Soul. Since I cannot now receive Thee sacramentally, come at least spiritually into my heart. As though Thou wert already there, I embrace Thee and unite myself wholly to Thee; permit not that I should ever be separated from Thee.[46]

Depending on the circumstances, if one needs a shorter prayer, or if one prefers a simpler form, the same saint proposes that we very simply say:

> O Jesus, I believe that You are present in the Blessed Sacrament; I love You and desire You. Come into my heart. I embrace You. Please never leave me.[47]

---

[44] St. Thomas Aquinas, *Summa Theologica*, IIIa, q. 80, a. 1, *ad* 3.
[45] Council of Trent, Session XIII, Decree Concerning the Sacrament of the Eucharist, ch. 8, in DZ 1648-1649.
[46] St. Alphonsus Liguori, *Visits to the Blessed Sacrament*, Apôtre du Foyer, 2000, p. 26.
[47] *Ibid.*, p. 27.

The Mysteries of the Rosary

Joyful Mysteries

First Mystery: The Annunciation by the Angel Gabriel to the Virgin Mary; intention for this mystery: humility.

Second Mystery: The Visitation of Our Lady to her cousin Elizabeth; intention for this mystery: fraternal charity.

Third Mystery: The Birth of Jesus in a stable; intention for this mystery: the spirit of poverty.

Fourth Mystery: The Presentation of the Child Jesus in the Temple: intention for this mystery: obedience and purity.

Fifth Mystery: The Finding of the Child Jesus in the Temple: intention for this mystery: to seek God in everything.

Sorrowful Mysteries

First Mystery: The Agony of Jesus in the Garden of Olives; intention for this mystery: contrition for our sins.

Second Mystery: The Scourging of Our Lord; intention for this mystery: mortification of the senses.

Third Mystery: The Crowning with Thorns; intention for this mystery: mortification of the mind and heart.

Fourth Mystery: The Carrying of the Cross: intention for this mystery: patience and perseverance in trials.

Fifth Mystery: The Crucifixion and Death of Jesus on the Cross: intention for this mystery: greater love for God and for souls.

Glorious Mysteries

First Mystery: The Resurrection of Our Lord; intention for this mystery: faith.

Second Mystery: The Ascension of Jesus into heaven; intention for this mystery: hope.

Third Mystery: The Descent of the Holy Ghost on the Blessed Virgin and the Apostles; intention for this mystery: missionary zeal.

Fourth Mystery: The Assumption of Our Lady into heaven: intention for this mystery: the grace of a happy death.

Fifth Mystery: The Coronation of Mary as Queen of Heaven: intention for this mystery: greater devotion to the Blessed Virgin.

The Apostles' Creed

I believe in God, the Father Almighty, Creator of heaven and earth;

and in Jesus Christ, His only Son, Our Lord,

Who was conceived by the Holy Ghost, born of the Virgin Mary,

suffered under Pontius Pilate, was crucified, died, and was buried.

He descended into hell; the third day He rose again from the dead;

He ascended into heaven, and sitteth at the right hand of God, the Father Almighty,

from thence He shall come to judge the living and the dead.

I believe in the Holy Ghost,
the holy Catholic Church, the communion of saints,
the forgiveness of sins,
the resurrection of the body,
and life everlasting. Amen.

An Act of Faith

O my God, I firmly believe that Thou art One God in Three Divine Persons: Father, Son, and Holy Ghost. I believe that Thy Divine Son became man and died for our sins, and that He shall come to judge the living and the dead. I believe these and all the truths which the Holy Catholic Church teaches because Thou hast revealed them, Who canst neither deceive nor be deceived.

An Act of Hope

O my God, relying on Thy almighty power and infinite mercy and promises, I hope to obtain pardon of my sins, the help of Thy grace, and life everlasting, through the merits of Jesus Christ, my Lord and Redeemer.

An Act of Charity

O my God, I love Thee above all things, with my whole heart and soul, because Thou art all-good and worthy of all love. I love my neighbor as myself for the love of Thee. I forgive all who have injured me and ask pardon of all whom I have injured.

An Act of Contrition

O my God, I am heartily sorry for having offended Thee. And I detest all my sins, because I dread the loss of heaven and the pains of hell, but most of all because I have offended Thee, my God, who art all good and deserving of all my love. I firmly resolve, with the help of Thy grace, to confess my sins, to do penance, and to amend my life.

The Memorare of St. Bernard

(1090-1153)

Remember, O most gracious Virgin Mary, that never was it known that anyone who fled to thy protection, implored thy help, or sought thy intercession, was left unaided. Inspired by this confidence, I fly unto thee, O Virgin of virgins, my Mother. To thee do I come, before thee I stand, sinful and sorrowful. O Mother of the Word Incarnate, despise not my petitions, but in thy mercy hear and answer me. Amen.

Litany of Humility

O Jesus! meek and humble of heart, *Hear me.*
From the desire of being esteemed, *Deliver me, Jesus.*
From the desire of being loved,
From the desire of being extolled,
From the desire of being honored,
From the desire of being praised,
From the desire of being preferred to others,
From the desire of being consulted,
From the desire of being approved,
From the fear of being humiliated, *Deliver me, Jesus.*
From the fear of being despised,
From the fear of suffering rebukes,
From the fear of being calumniated,
From the fear of being forgotten,
From the fear of being ridiculed,
From the fear of being wronged,
From the fear of being suspected,
That others may be loved more than I, *Jesus, grant me the grace to desire it.*
That others may be esteemed more than I,
That, in the opinion of the world,

That others may increase and I may decrease,
That others may be chosen and I set aside,
That others may be praised and I unnoticed,
That others may be preferred to me in everything,
That others may become holier than I, provided that I may become as holy as I should…

Litany of the Precious Blood

Lord, have mercy. *Lord, have mercy.*
Christ, have mercy. *Christ, have mercy.*
Lord, have mercy. *Lord, have mercy.*
Christ, hear us. *Christ, hear us.*
Christ, graciously hear us. *Christ, graciously hear us.*
God, the Father of heaven, *have mercy on us.*
God the Son, Redeemer of the world,
God, the Holy Ghost,
Holy Trinity, one God
Blood of Christ, only-begotten Son of the Eternal Father,
    Save us.
Blood of Christ, Incarnate Word of God,
Blood of Christ, of the New and Eternal Testament,
Blood of Christ, falling upon the earth in the Agony,
Blood of Christ, shed profusely in the Scourging,
Blood of Christ, flowing forth in the Crowning with Thorns,
Blood of Christ, poured out on the Cross,
Blood of Christ, price of our salvation,
Blood of Christ, without which there is no forgiveness,
Blood of Christ, Eucharistic drink and refreshment of souls,
Blood of Christ, stream of mercy,
Blood of Christ, victor over demons,
Blood of Christ, courage of Martyrs,
Blood of Christ, strength of Confessors,
Blood of Christ, bringing forth Virgins,

Blood of Christ, help of those in peril,
Blood of Christ, relief of the burdened,
Blood of Christ, solace in sorrow,
Blood of Christ, hope of the penitent,
Blood of Christ, consolation of the dying,
Blood of Christ, peace and tenderness of hearts,
Blood of Christ, pledge of eternal life,
Blood of Christ, freeing souls from purgatory,
Blood of Christ, most worthy of all glory and honor,
Lamb of God, who takest away the sins of the world, *spare us, O Lord.*

Lamb of God, who takest away the sins of the world, *graciously hear us, O Lord.*

Lamb of God, who takest away the sins of the world, *have mercy on us, O Lord.*

V. Thou hast redeemed us, O Lord, in Thy Blood.
R. And made us a kingdom for our God.

Let us pray: Almighty and eternal God, Thou hast appointed Thine only-begotten Son the Redeemer of the world, and wast willing to be appeased by His Blood. Grant, we beseech Thee, that we may worthily adore this price of our salvation, and through its power be safeguarded from the evils of the present life, so that we may rejoice in its fruits forever in heaven. Through the same Christ, our Lord. Amen.

Litany of the Sacred Heart

Lord, have mercy. *Lord, have mercy.*
Christ, have mercy. *Christ, have mercy.*
Lord, have mercy. *Lord, have mercy.*
Christ, hear us. *Christ, hear us.*
Christ, graciously hear us. *Christ, graciously hear us.*
God the Father of heaven, *have mercy on us.*
God the Son, Redeemer of the world,
God the Holy Ghost,
Holy Trinity, one God,
Heart of Jesus, Son of the Eternal Father,
Heart of Jesus, formed by the Holy Ghost in the womb of the Virgin Mother,
Heart of Jesus, substantially united to the Word of God,
Heart of Jesus, of Infinite Majesty.
Heart of Jesus, sacred Temple of God,
Heart of Jesus, Tabernacle of the Most High,
Heart of Jesus, House of God and Gate of heaven,
Heart of Jesus, burning furnace of charity,
Heart of Jesus, abode of justice and love,
Heart of Jesus, full of goodness and love,
Heart of Jesus, abyss of all virtues,
Heart of Jesus, most worthy of all praise,
Heart of Jesus, King and center of all hearts,
Heart of Jesus, in whom are all treasures of wisdom and knowledge,
Heart of Jesus, in whom dwells the fullness of divinity,
Heart of Jesus, in whom the Father was well pleased,
Heart of Jesus, of whose fullness we have all received,
Heart of Jesus, desire of the everlasting hills,
Heart of Jesus, patient and most merciful,
Heart of Jesus, enriching all who invoke Thee,
Heart of Jesus, fountain of life and holiness,
Heart of Jesus, propitiation for our sins,
Heart of Jesus, loaded down with opprobrium,

Heart of Jesus, bruised for our offenses, *have mercy on us.*
Heart of Jesus, obedient to death,
Heart of Jesus, pierced with a lance,
Heart of Jesus, source of all consolation,
Heart of Jesus, our life and resurrection,
Heart of Jesus, our peace and our reconciliation,
Heart of Jesus, victim for our sins,
Heart of Jesus, salvation of those who trust in Thee,
Heart of Jesus, hope of those who die in Thee,
Heart of Jesus, delight of all the Saints,
Lamb of God, who takest away the sins of the world, *spare us, O Lord.*

Lamb of God, who takest away the sins of the world, *graciously hear us, O Lord.*

Lamb of God, who takest away the sins of the world, *have mercy on us, O Lord.*

V. Jesus, meek and humble of heart,
R. Make our hearts like unto Thine.

Let us pray: Almighty and eternal God, look upon the Heart of Thy most beloved Son and upon the praises and satisfaction which He offers Thee in the name of sinners; and to those who implore Thy mercy, in Thy great goodness, grant forgiveness in the name of the same Jesus Christ, Thy Son, who liveth and reigneth with Thee forever and ever. Amen.

Magnificat (Canticle, Luke 1:46-55)

*Magnificat * anima mea Dominum:*

My soul doth magnify the Lord.

*et exsultavit spiritus meus * in Deo salutari meo.*

And my spirit hath rejoiced in God my Saviour.

*Quia respexit humilitatem ancillæ suæ: * ecce enim ex hoc beatam me dicent omnes generationes,*

Because He hath regarded the humility of His handmaid; for behold from henceforth all generations shall call me blessed.

*quia fecit mihi magna qui potens est: * et sanctum nomen ejus,*

Because He that is mighty, hath done great things to me; and holy is His name.

*et misericordia ejus a progenie in progenies * timentibus eum.*

And His mercy is from generation unto generations, to them that fear Him.

*Fecit potentiam in brachio suo: * dispersit superbos mente cordis sui.*

He hath shewed might in His arm: He hath scattered the proud in the conceit of their heart.

*Deposuit potentes de sede, * et exaltavit humiles.*

He hath put down the mighty from their seat, and hath exalted the humble.

*Esurientes implevit bonis: * et divites dimisit inanes.*

He hath filled the hungry with good things; and the rich He hath sent empty away.

*Suscepit Israël puerum suum, * recordatus misericordiæ suæ:*

He hath received Israel His servant, being mindful of His mercy:

*sicut locutus est ad patres nostros, * Abraham et semini ejus in sæcula*

As He spoke to our fathers, to Abraham and to his seed for ever.

*Gloria Patri et Filio, * et Spiritui Sancto,*

Glory be to the Father, and to the Son, and to the Holy Ghost,

Sicut erat in principio, et nunc et semper, * et in saecula saeculorum. Amen.

as it was in the beginning, is now, and ever shall be, world without end. Amen.

Stabat Mater (Sequence)

*Stabat Mater dolorosa
Juxta crucem lacrimosa
Dum pendebat Filius.*

At the cross, her station keeping,
Stood the mournful Mother weeping,
Close to Jesus to the last.

*Cujus animam gementem
Contristatam et dolentem
Pertransivit gladius.*

Through her heart, His sorrow sharing,
All His bitter anguish bearing,
Now at length the sword had passed.

*O quam tristis et afflicta
Fuit illa benedicta
Mater Unigeniti!*

Oh, how sad and sore distressèd
Was that Mother highly blessèd
Of the sole-begotten One!

*Quae maerebat et dolebat
Pia Mater dum videbat
Nati poenas inclyti.*

Christ above in torment hangs,
She beneath beholds the pangs
Of her dying, glorious Son.

*Quis est homo qui non fleret
Matrem Christi si videret
In tanto supplicio?*

Is there one who would not weep,
Whelmed in miseries so deep,
Christ's dear Mother to behold?

*Quis non posset contristari
Christi Matrem contemplari
Dolentem cum Filio?*

Can the human heart refrain
From partaking in her pain,
In that Mother's pain untold?

*Pro peccatis suae gentis
Vidit Jesum in tormentis
Et flagellis subditum.*

Bruised, derided, cursed, defiled,
She beheld her tender Child,
All with bloody scourges rent.

*Vidit suum dulcem natum
Moriendo desolatum
Dum emisit spiritum.*

For the sins of His own nation
Saw Him hang in desolation
Till His spirit forth He sent.

*Eia Mater, fons amoris,
Me sentire vim doloris
Fac ut tecum lugeam.*

O sweet mother! Font of love,
Touch my spirit from above,
Make my heart with thine accord.

Bibliography

Sacred Scripture

Acts: Acts of the Apostles
Apoc: Book of the Apocalypse
Col: Epistle of St. Paul to the Colossians
Eph: Epistle of St. Paul to the Ephesians
Ex: Book of Exodus
Gal: Epistle of St. Paul to the Galatians
Gen: Genesis
Heb: Epistle of St. Paul to the Hebrews
Is: Book of the Prophet Isaias
Jn: Gospel according to St. John
Job: Book of Job
Lk: Gospel according to St. Luke
Lam: Book of Lamentations of Jeremias
Mt: Gospel according to St. Matthew
Phil: Epistle of St. Paul to the Philippians
Prov: Proverbs
Ps: Psalm
Sir: Sirach, Book of Ecclesiasticus
Zach: Book of the Prophet Zacharias
I Cor: First Epistle of St. Paul to the Corinthians
II Cor: Second Epistle of St. Paul to the Corinthians
I Tim: First Epistle of St. Paul to Timothy
II Tim: Second Epistle of St. Paul to Timothy

St. Alphonsus Liguori

SSJ: *La Sainteté au jour le jour* (Clovis, 2014).

St. Angela of Foligno

Visions et révélations (Namur: éditions du Soleil levant, 1958).

St. Basil

S: *Sermon I sur la vertu et le vice*, in: *Oeuvres complètes*, vol. III/2 (Paris: Gaume, 1839).

St. Benedict

PPJ: *Une pensée par jour*, compiled by Sister Véronique Dupont, O.S.B. (Médiaspaul, 2007).

St. Bernadette

CNI: *Le Carnet de notes intimes* (1873-1874), in *Les écrits de sainte Bernadette et sa voie spirituelle* (Lethielleux, 1980).

L: *Lettres* (1873-1875), in *Les écrits de sainte Bernadette et sa voie spirituelle* (Lethielleux, 1980).

PPJ: *Une pensée par jour*, compiled by Pascal Frey (Médiaspaul, 2012).

St. Catherine of Siena

D: *Le Dialogue* (Téqui, 1976).

R: *Le Rosaire*, texts by St. Catherine of Siena (Monastère de Chambarand, 2001).

Charles de Foucauld

NQ: *Notes quotidiennes*.

PPJ: *Une pensée par jour*, compiled by Patrice Mahieu, O.S.B. (Médiaspaul, 2010).

Clement of Alexandria

Stromata, book II, chapter 4.

Clement XI

General prayer, "Thanksgiving after Mass," in *Diurnale romanum*, 1960.

[Curé of Ars: see St. John Vianney]

St. Cyprian

UE: *De l'Unité de l'Église catholique*, coll. Unam sanctam (Paris: Cerf, 1942).

St. Cyril of Jerusalem

Catechetical Lectures, Nicene and Post-Nicene Fathers, 2nd series, vol. 7.

Elizabeth of the Trinity

L: *Oeuvres complètes, Lettres du Carmel*, vol. 1 (Cerf, 1980).

PPJ: *Une pensée par jour*, compiled by the Carmelites of Dijon (Médiaspaul, 2006).

St. Francis de Sales
PPJ: *Une pensée par jour*, compiled by Sister Marie-Christophe, Visitation Monastery, Voiron (Médiaspaul, 2008).

St. Francis Xavier
PPJ: *Une pensée par jour*, compiled by Nicolas Rousselot (Médiaspaul, 2015).

St. Gregory the Great
PPJ: *Une pensée par jour*, compiled by Jacqueline Martin-Bagnaudez (Médiaspaul, 2012).

Blessed Henry Suso
GLL: *Grand Livre des lettres*, Letter 24.
LS: *Livre de la Sagesse* éternelle.

St. Ignatius of Antioch
EpE: *Epistle of St. Ignatius to the Ephesians*, Ante-Nicene Fathers, vol. 1.

St. Jacinta of Fatima
MSL: *Mémoires de soeur Lucie* (Téqui, 1991).

St. Jeanne de Chantal
R: *Le Rosaire, textes de sainte Jeanne de Chantal* (Monastère de Chambarand, 2005).

St. Joan of France
R. Le Rosaire, textes de sainte Jeanne de France (Monastère de Chambarand, 2001).

St. John Bosco
MDB: *Massime del Beato Don Bosco* (Turin: Soc. Ed. Internazionale, 1929).
PDB: *I Pensieri di Don Bosco* (Turin: Edizioni Elledici, 1998).

St. John Climacus
The Ladder of Divine Ascent

St. John Vianney, the Curé of Ars

- MR: *Ma Rosaire avec le saint curé d'Ars* (Téqui, 1932).
- PPJ1: *Une pensée par jour* (Clovis, 2006).
- PPJ2: *Une pensée par jour*, compiled by Claudine Fearon (Médiaspaul, 2010).

St. Maximilian Kolbe

- CSm: *Carnets spirituels (Méditations quotidiennes)*, French translation by Fr. Grémaud, M.S.C. (Lethielleux, 1981).

Blessed Pauline Jaricot

- PPJ: *Une pensée par jour*, compiled by Oeuvres Pontificales missionnaires (Lyons), (Médiaspaul, 2008).

St. Peter Julian Eymard

- PPJ: *Une pensée par jour*, compiled by Sister Suzanne Aylwin (Médiaspaul, 2010).

St. Pius X

Prières et oeuvres pies (Marietti, 1938).

Padre Pio

- ASN: Angela Serritelli, *Notizie su Padre Pio*, in Archives Padre Pio.
- FFN: Filomena Fini, *Notizie su Padre Pio*, in APP.
- GB: Giovanni da Baggio, *Padre Pio visto dall'interno* (Firenze 1970).
- PPJ: *Une pensée par jour*, compiled by Father Gerardo Di Flumeri, O.F.M. Cap. (Médiaspaul, 2010).

St. Teresa of Avila

- Ch P: *Le Chemin de la Perfection* in *Oeuvres complètes* (Seuil, 1949).

St. Thérèse of the Child Jesus

- PPJ: *Une pensée par jour*, compiled by Hélène Mongin (Médiaspaul, 2012).
- PC: *Procès canonique*, 1915-1917 (Rome: Teresianum, 1976).

St. Thomas Aquinas

Commentaire sur les psaumes (Cerf, 1996).

PPJ: *Une pensée par jour*, compiled by Agnès Jauréguibéhère (Médiaspaul, 2012).

Summa Theologiae

St. Vincent de Paul

X: "Entretiens aux Filles de la Charité," in *St. Vincent de Paul: correspondance, entretiens, documents*, vol. X (Librairie Lecoffre, J. Gabalda Éd., 1923).

XII: "Entretiens au prêtres de la Mission," in *St. Vincent de Paul: correspondance, entretiens, documents*, vol. XII (Librairie Lecoffre, J. Gabalda Éd., 1924).

PPJ: *Une pensée par jour*, compiled by Father Jean-Yves Ducoumeau (Médiaspaul, 2007).

Other Authors

ACP: *L'Ami du clergé paroissial* (Imprimerie Maitrier et Courtot, 1903).

COE: Alberigo, ed., *Les Conciles oecuméniques*, vol. II (Paris: Cerf, 1994).

OEO: Bossuet, *Oeuvres oratoires*, vols. II and IV (Paris: Desclée de Brouwer, 1891 and 1892)

OEC: Bourdaloue, *Oeuvres complètes* (Guérin, 1864), vol. II.

365J: Father Calmel, *365 jours avec le père Calmel*, unpublished manuscript, finished in May 2014.

R: Père Chevrier, *Le Rosaire, textes du père Chevrier* (Monastère de Chamarand, 2001).

VF: Monseigneur Chevrot, *Les Petites Vertus du foyer* (Le Laurier, 2001); *Homélie, À l'écoute du Seigneur*, cassette no. 6, Téqui.

SMP: Monseigneur Cimichella, *Sainte Françoise-Xavier Cabrini, soeur Mouvement Perpétuel* (Montreal: Jésus-Marie, 1981).

Au. S.: Léon de Clary, *L'Auréole séraphique*, vols. I and IV (Paris: Bloud et Barral, 1882).

AS: Père Cormier, *Une Année avec les saints* (Avrillé: Sel, 2008).

Bibliography

M: Père Emmanuel, *Méditations pour tous les jours de l'année liturgique* (Dismas, 1987).

ID: Père Gabriel de Sainte Marie-Madeleine, O.C.D., *Intimité divine* (Monastère des carmélites déchaussées, Alost, Belgium, 1957, 1958, or 1961 depending on the volume).

AL: Dom Guéranger, *L'Année liturgique: le temps de l'Avent* (TA), (H. Oudin, 1876). *Le temps de Noël* (TN), *la Septuagésime* (Sept.), (H. Oudin, 1878).

Pa. S.:   *Le Palmier séraphique*, vol. III, *mars*, ed. Monseigneur Guérin (Librairie Guérin, 1872-1873).

PB: Monseigneur Guérin, *Les Petits Bollandistes*, vol. I (1 – 26 janvier) (Bloud et Barral, 1876).

PG: Migne, *Patrologie grecque*.

PL: Migne, *Patrologie latine*.

PS: Alain Mius, *Prier avec les saints: recueil de litanies,* vols. I, II, and III (Résiac, 2005, 2006, 2014).

E: Père Daniel-Antonin Mortier, O.P., *L'Évangile: simples commentaires pour la vie chrétienne* (Paris: Desclée de Brouwer et Cie., 1925).

CV: Monseigneur Louis Soubigou, *La Croix au coeur de notre vie* (Lethielleux, 1957).

LP (Pastoral letters)

    Bishop Joseph Giray, Bishop of Cahors, *Le Vénérable Alain de Solminihac*, 1928.

    Bishop Joseph Lefebvre, *Jeanne de France*, Bourges, 1950.

    Bishop Joseph Rumeau, *Bienheureux Noël Pinot*, Angers, 1926.

    Bishop Pierre-Marie Théas, *Sainte Bernadette*, Tarbes, 1954.

Other works cited

    Jacques Baudoin, *Grand livre des saints* (Créer, 2006).

    Père Chastenet, *La Vie de Mgr Alain de Solminihac* (1663).

    Abbé Dunand, *Histoires choisies des Pères des déserts d'Orient* (Édouard Privat, 1894).

Ernest Hello, *Physionomies de saints* (Variétés, 1945).

Père Léon, *Vie des saints … de saint François*, in: *Histoires choisies…* (Édouard Privat, 1894)

Ammien Marcellin, *Res gestae*, Book 23.

Pascale Moulier, *La Peinture religieuse en Haute-Auvergne* (Créer, 2007).

The Imitation of Christ.